Nature's Finest Cross Stitch Patterns
Collection 9

StitchX Cross Stitch Designs

GENERAL STITCHING INSTRUCTIONS

When purchasing your fabric for your cross stitch designs, you may wish to choose white or antique white fabric, or you might choose a complementary color to the design. Hand dyed fabrics are an excellent choice as well.

The finished design size is shown above the floss key. Be sure to add about 6 to 8 inches to each dimension so that you will have plenty of room for matting and framing.

For example, if the design size is 10" x 14", purchase fabric that is at least 16" x 20". If possible, serge or zig zag the edges of your fabric before beginning stitching.

Most stitchers prefer to start designs in the middle. To do so, fold your fabric in half vertically and horizontally. The intersection of the two folds is the approximate middle of your fabric. Find the center of your design by looking for the 'center arrows' and following them until they intersect. This will be the center of the design. Start stitching this area near the center mark on your fabric.

For solid designs (completely stitched from corner to corner), you can also easily start in one corner if you wish to. To do this, measure our fabric and decide how much extra you have on each side. If your fabric is 8 inches wider than your design, then you have 4 inches on each side of your design horizontally. Next, measure how tall your fabric is. Again, decide how much extra you have on the top and bottom. We recommend 4 inches on each side. Once you have determined how much extra you have, measure in from the corner you wish to start. This is where you will begin stitching. Make sure you have the correct page according to your page layout.

On larger designs, you will see that on some pages, there may be some greyed out boxes. If you see the greyed out areas, these are an overlap of the adjacent page (whether to the side or top or bottom). For example, if you see a page with the grey stitches on the right columns, you will know that another page goes to the right of that page. If you see a page that NOT have a greyed edge on the right, then that is the far right page of the pattern. Similarly, if you see a page with 3 grey rows on the bottom, you will know another page will go below it. If you have a page that does NOT have grey rows on the bottom, you will know that page belongs on the bottom row.

Here's an example: Imagine you have a chart with 6 pages. Start with page 1 in the upper left corner. Continue adding pages to the right until you ge to a page that does not have grey columns. Then start the next row. Again, continue until you ge to the end of the row. When you finish laying out your pages, you will see that you have either 2 rows of 3 pages, or 3 rows of 2 pages, depending on the layout of the design.

If possible, print (or copy) 2 of each page of the pattern. Use one for a master copy and one for marking up as needed. With your master copy, layout all pages and tape together before stitching. Use this set as a reference. Using your working copy, find the page that you will start stitching and use it to mark with a highlighter or pencil as you stitch. When you have finished a large section or a full page, be sure to mark that section out on your master copy. You'll see your progress!

We typically recommend using two strands of DMC floss for full stitches and fractional stitches. Backstitching (if any) is stitched with one strand of floss.

We do hope you enjoy stitching this pattern as much as we've enjoyed creating it.

ENJOY!

Please respect copyright law and do not share, email, trade, sell, or distribute this pattern in any way. The purchaser of this pattern is allowed to make a working copy as needed. Purchaser also has the right to sell finished projects created with this pattern.

Please visit us at www.xstitchpatterns.com where you can see our full range of patterns and/or contact us if necessary.

www.xstitchpatterns.com

Nature's Finest Cross Stitch Pattern

Stitch Count: 280 x 224
Finished Size on 14ct Aida: 20" x 16"

www.stitchx.com

Chart Page Number 1 — Nature's Finest No. 041

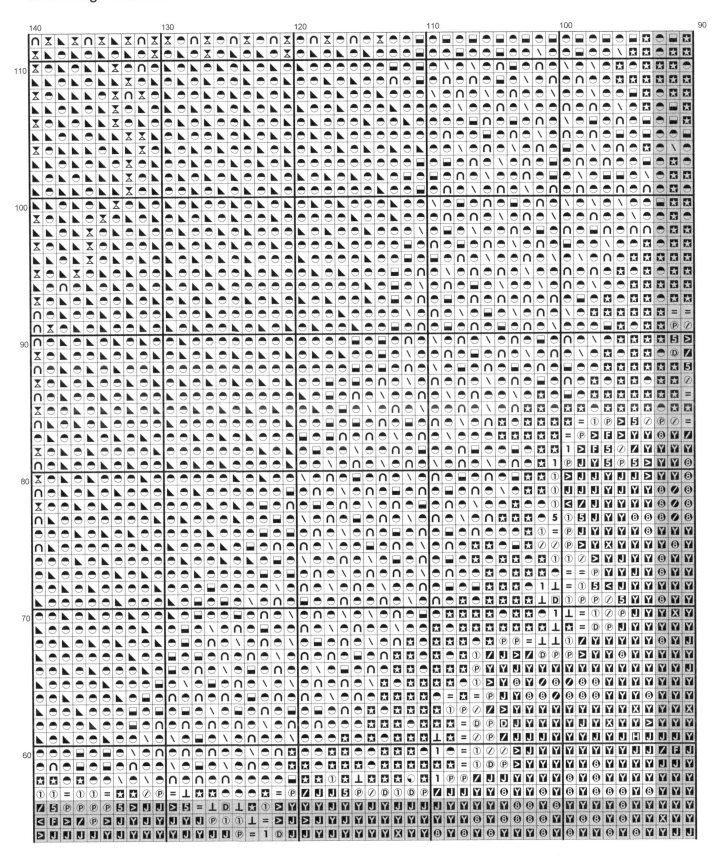

Chart Page Number 2 Nature's Finest No. 041

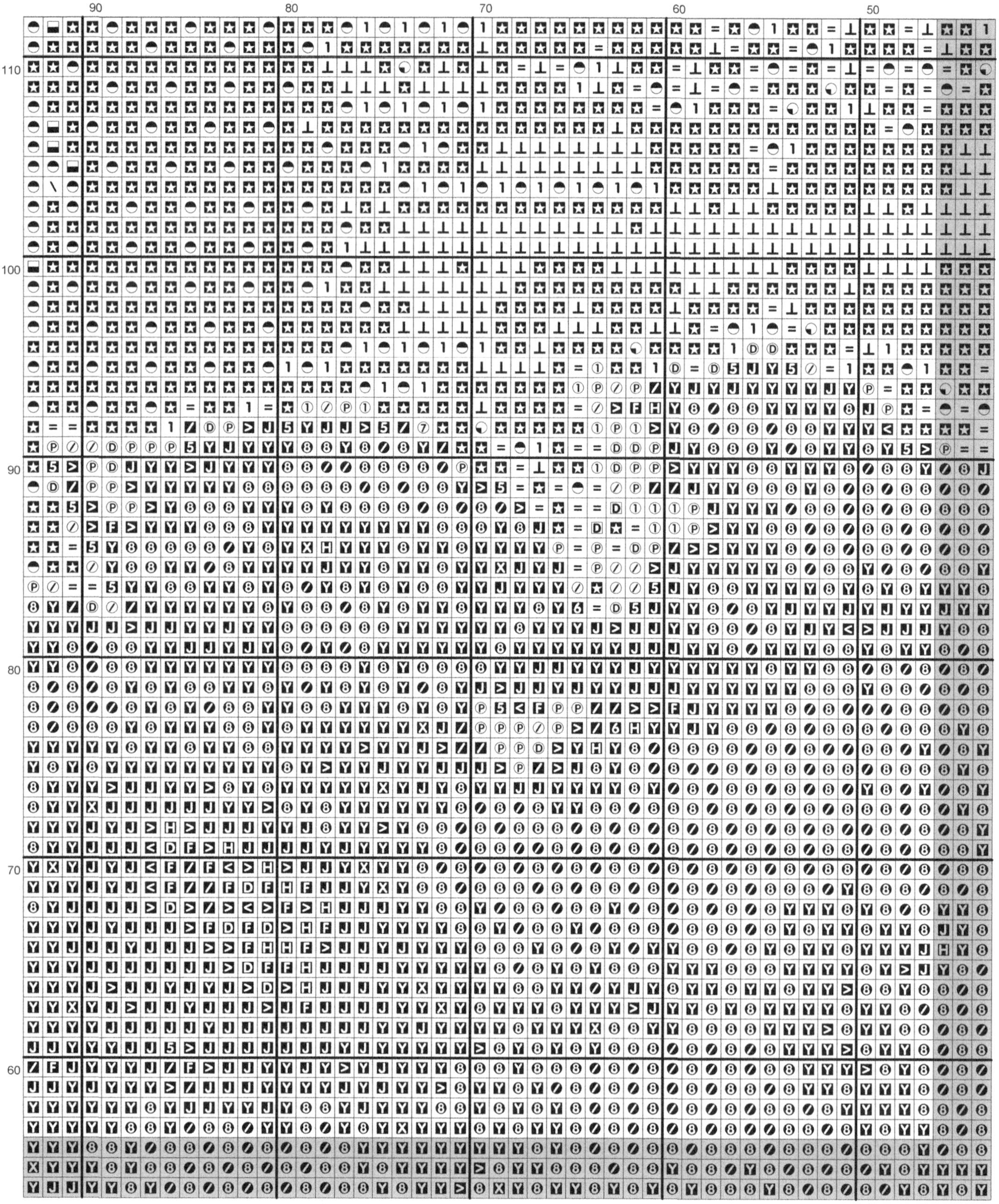

Chart Page Number 3   Nature's Finest No. 041

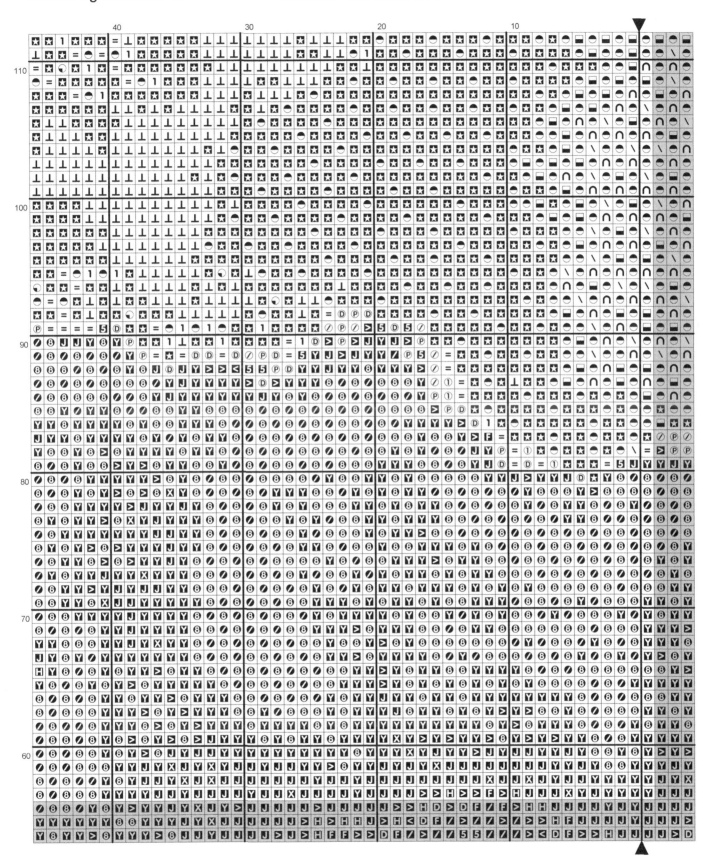

Chart Page Number 4 Nature's Finest No. 041

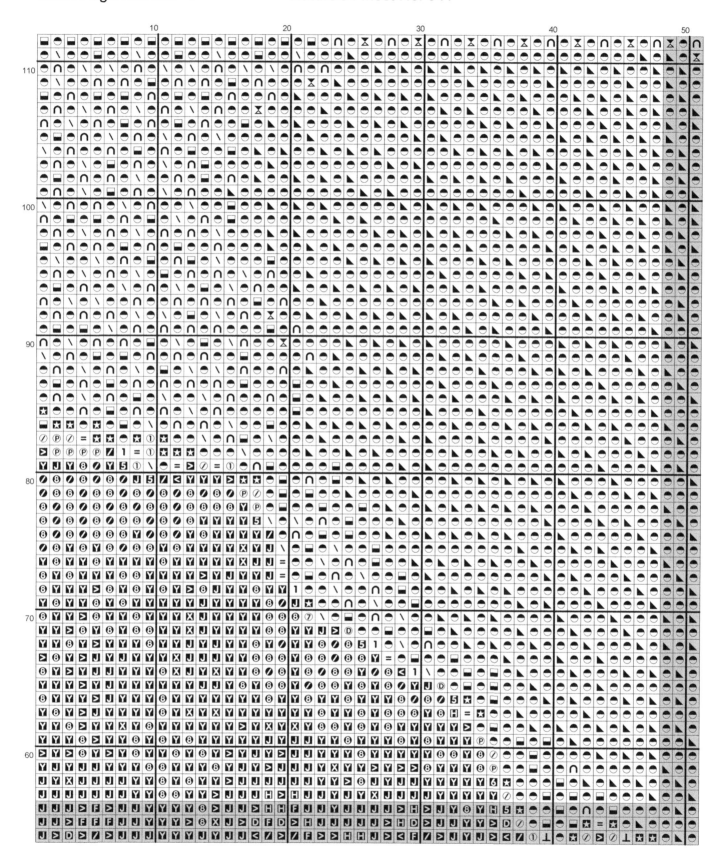

Chart Page Number 5　　Nature's Finest No. 041

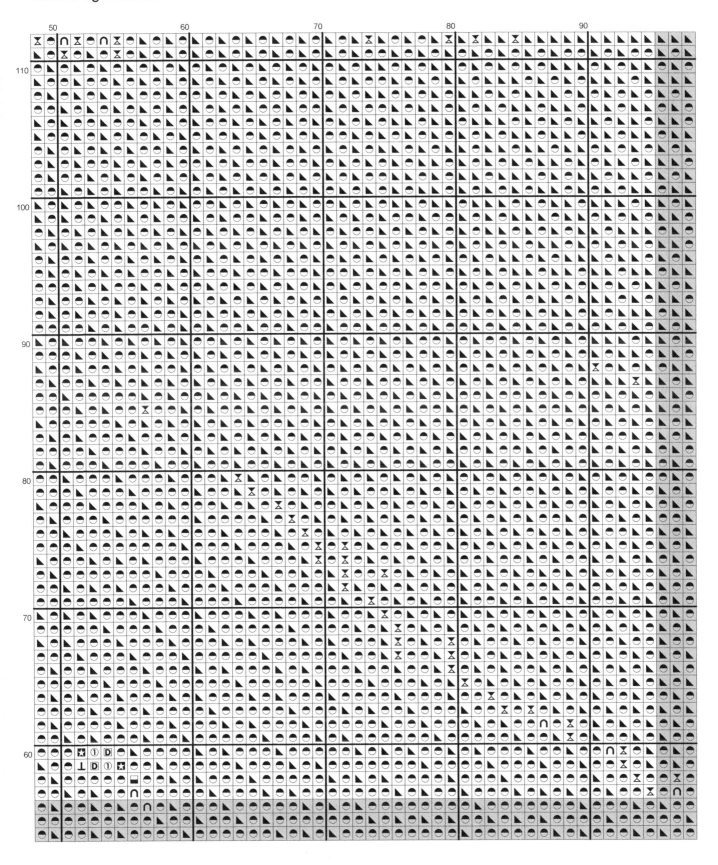

Chart Page Number 6 Nature's Finest No. 041

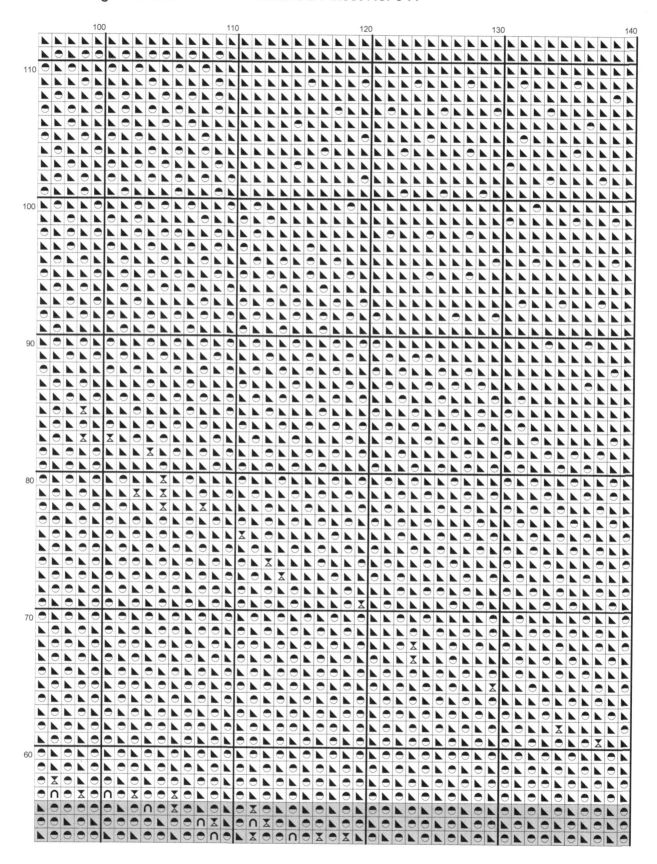

Chart Page Number 7   Nature's Finest No. 041

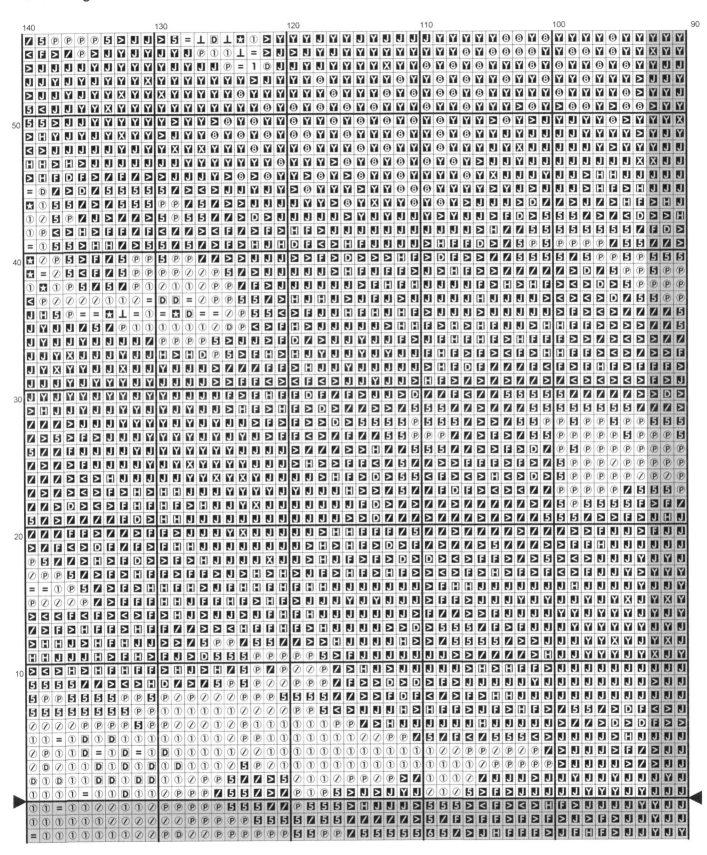

Chart Page Number 8   Nature's Finest No. 041

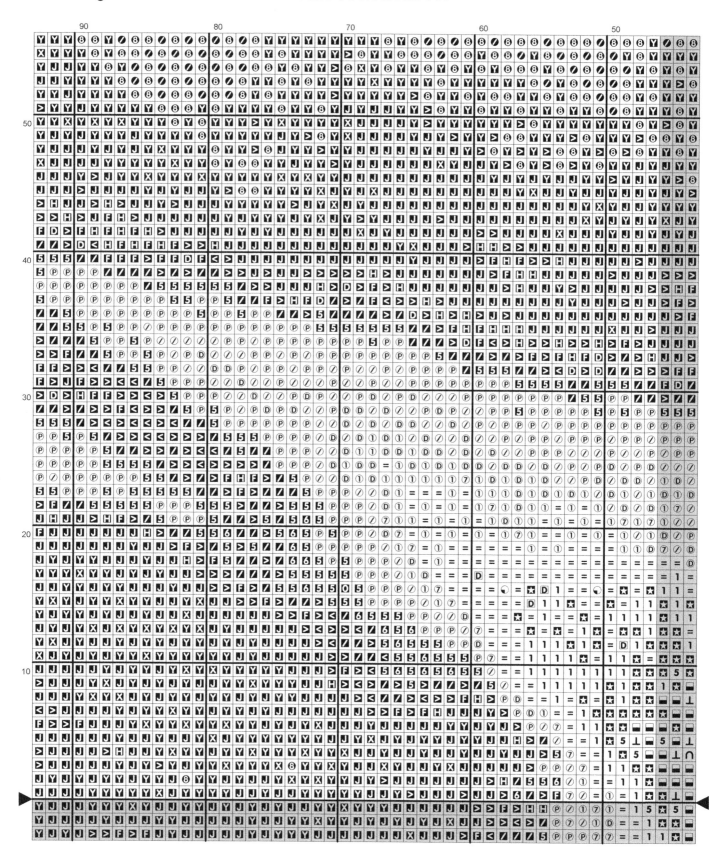

Chart Page Number 9

Nature's Finest No. 041

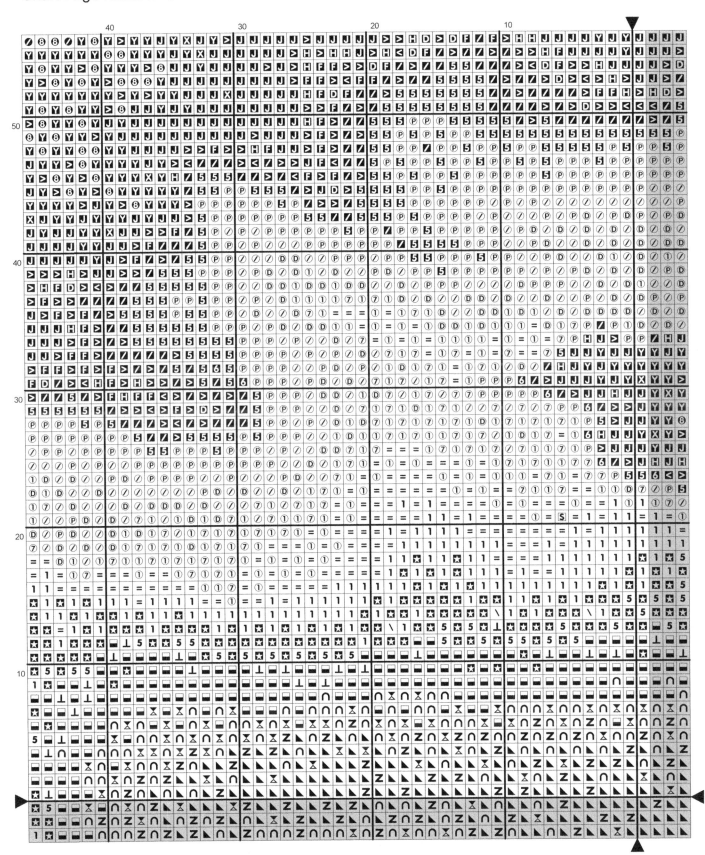

Chart Page Number 10   Nature's Finest No. 041

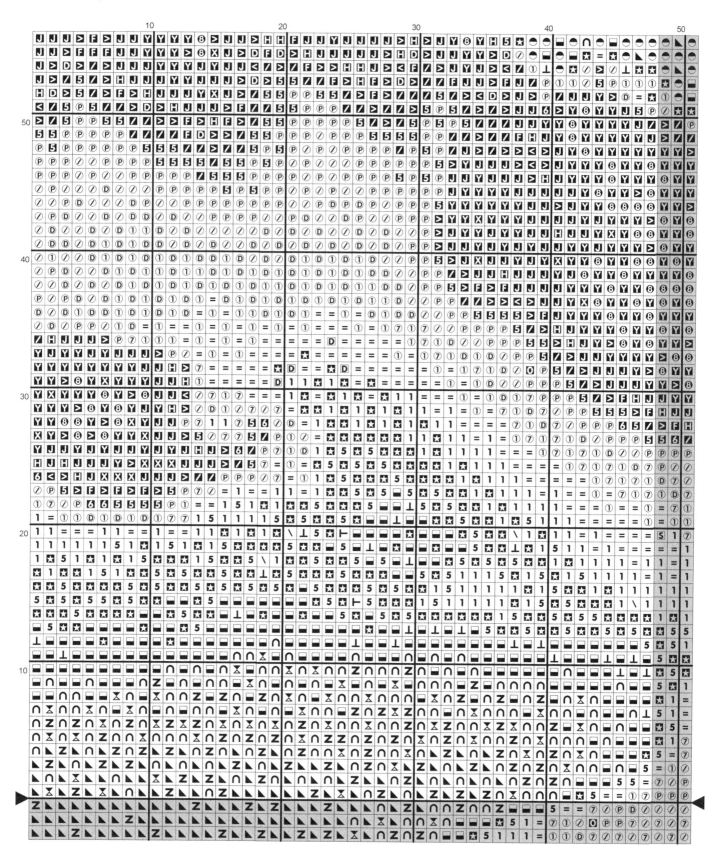

Chart Page Number 11 — Nature's Finest No. 041

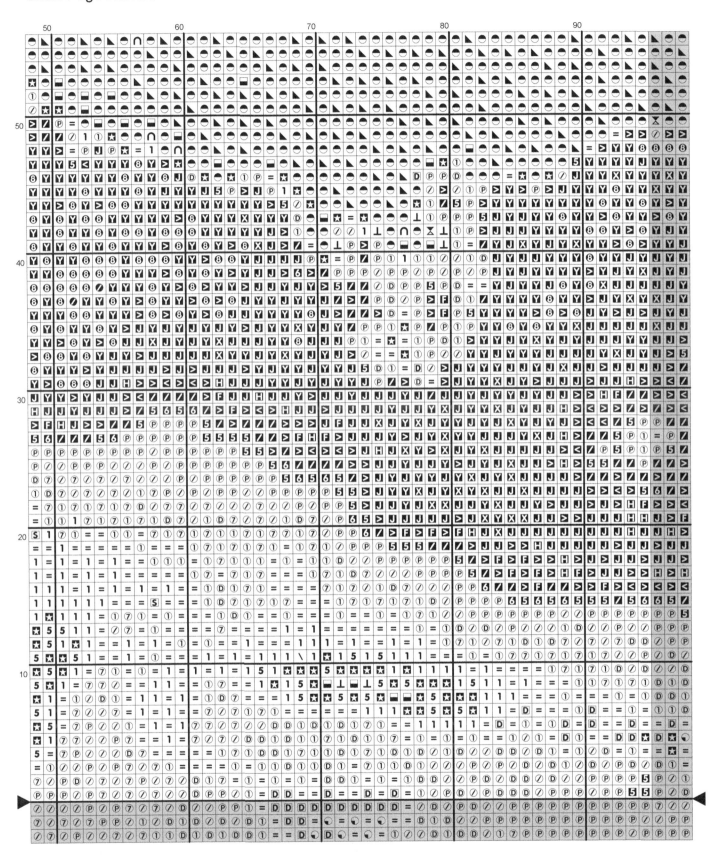

Chart Page Number 12 Nature's Finest No. 041

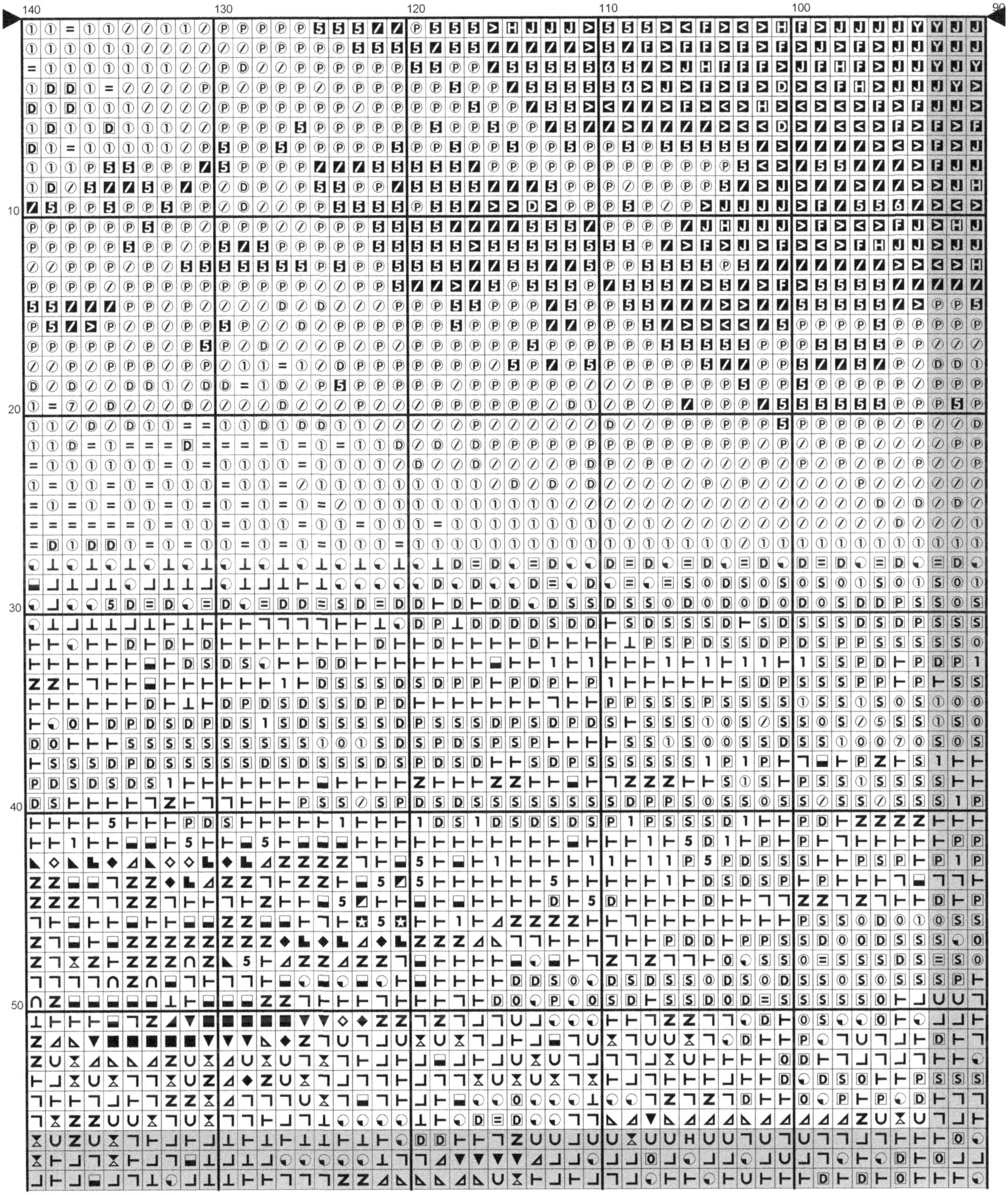

Chart Page Number 14   Nature's Finest No. 041

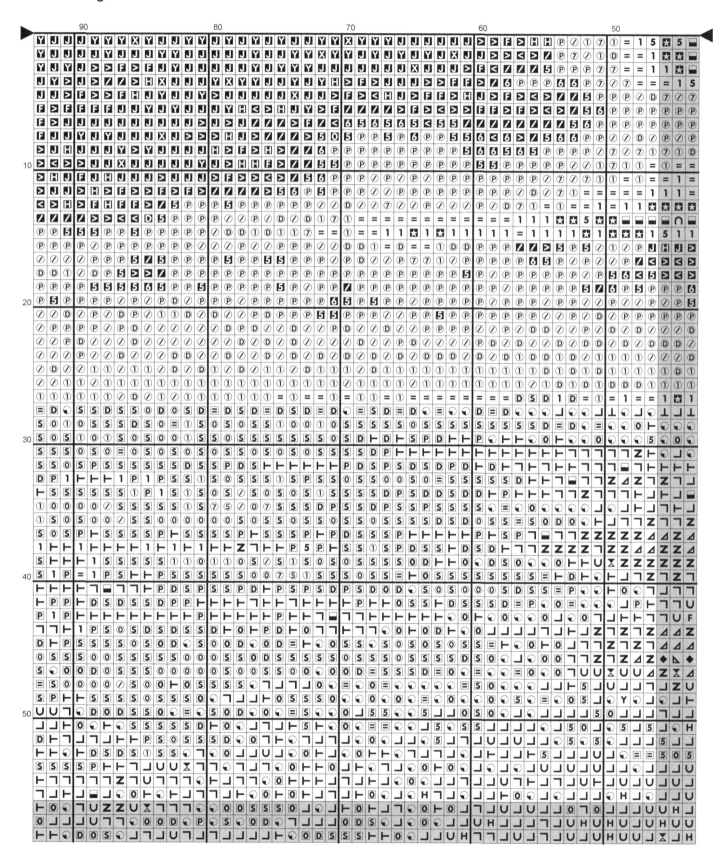

Chart Page Number 15 — Nature's Finest No. 041

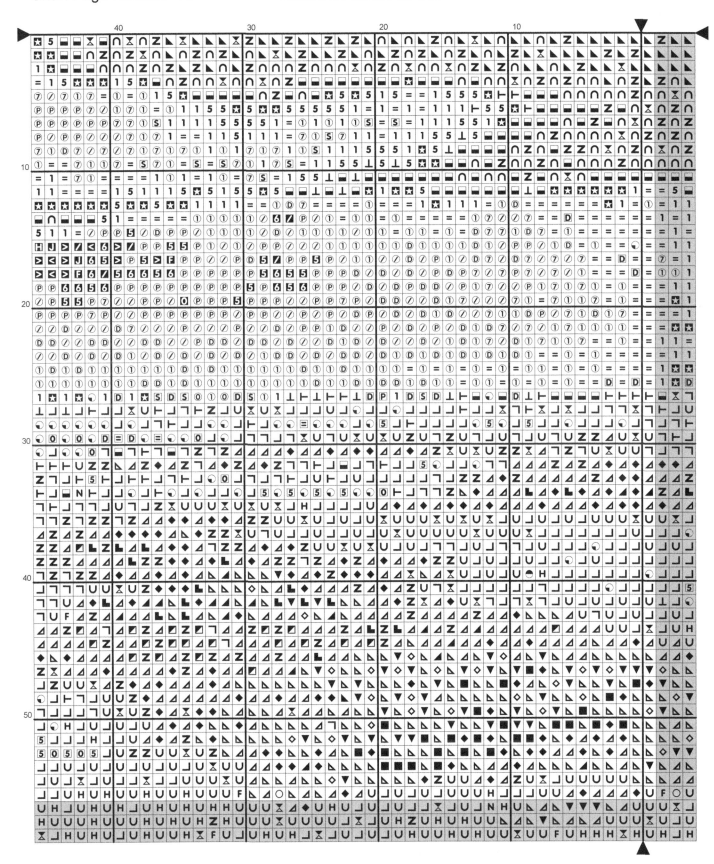

Chart Page Number 16   Nature's Finest No. 041

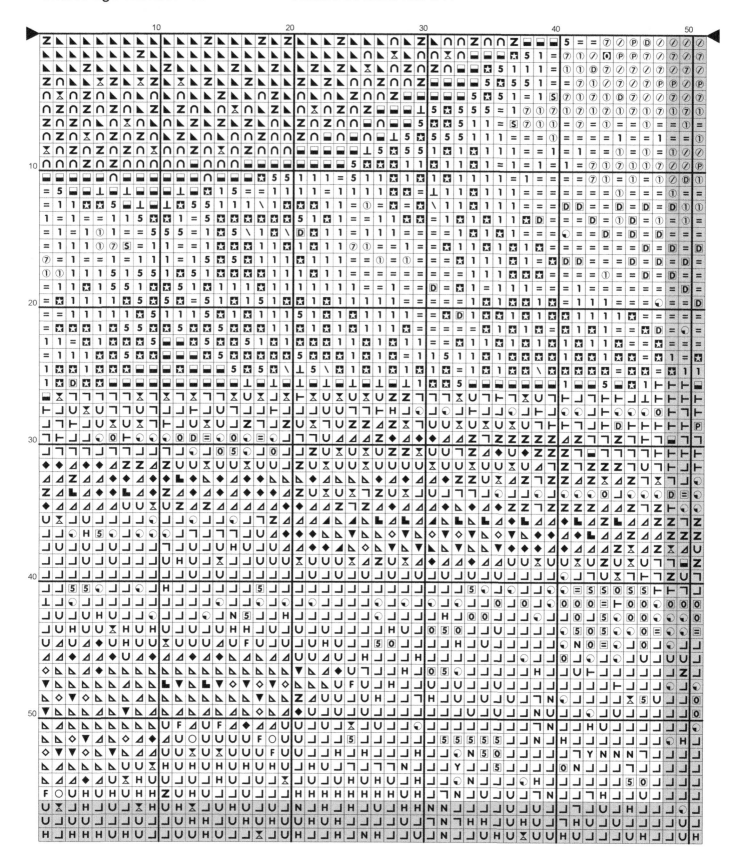

Chart Page Number 17   Nature's Finest No. 041

Chart Page Number 18 Nature's Finest No. 041

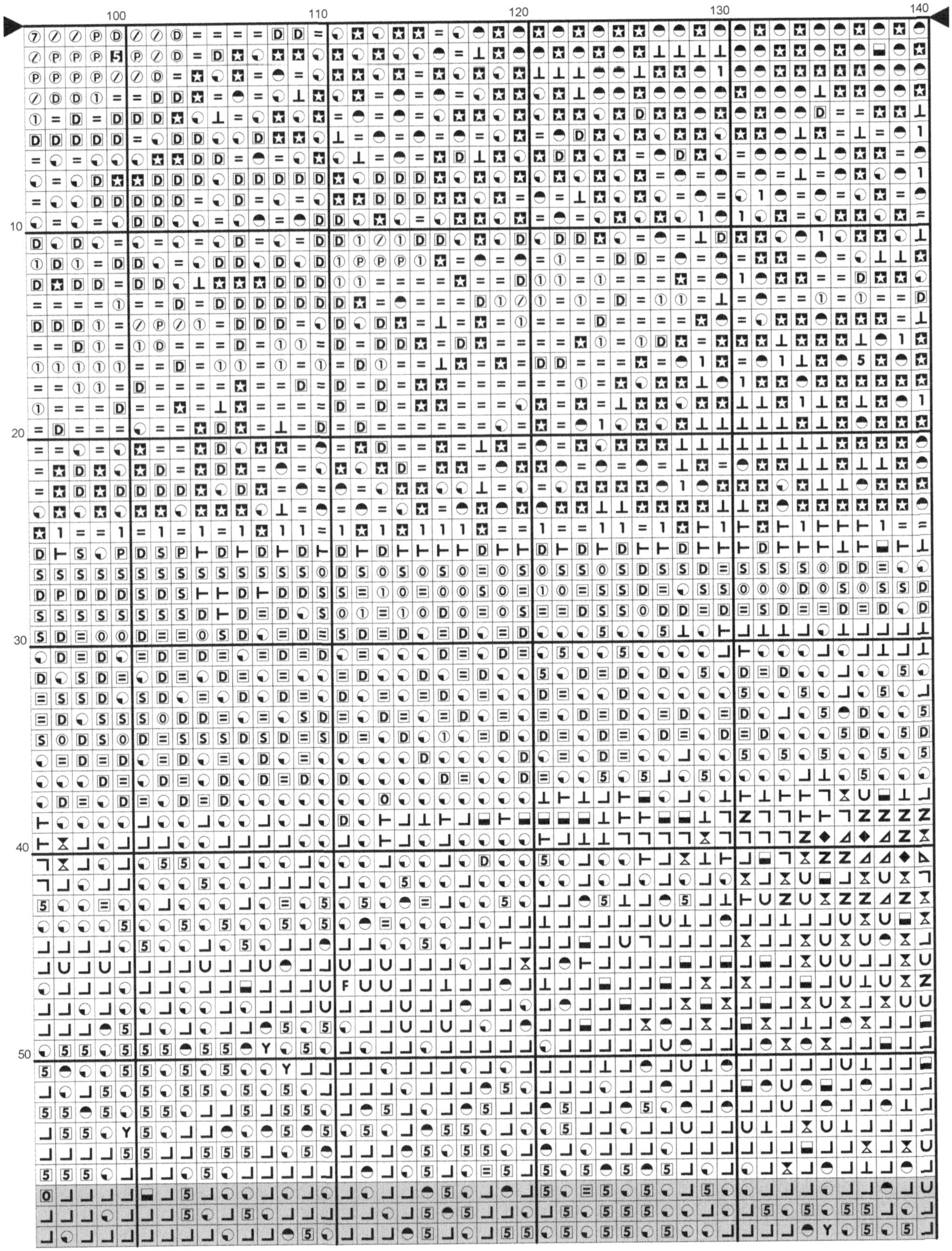

Chart Page Number 19   Nature's Finest No. 041

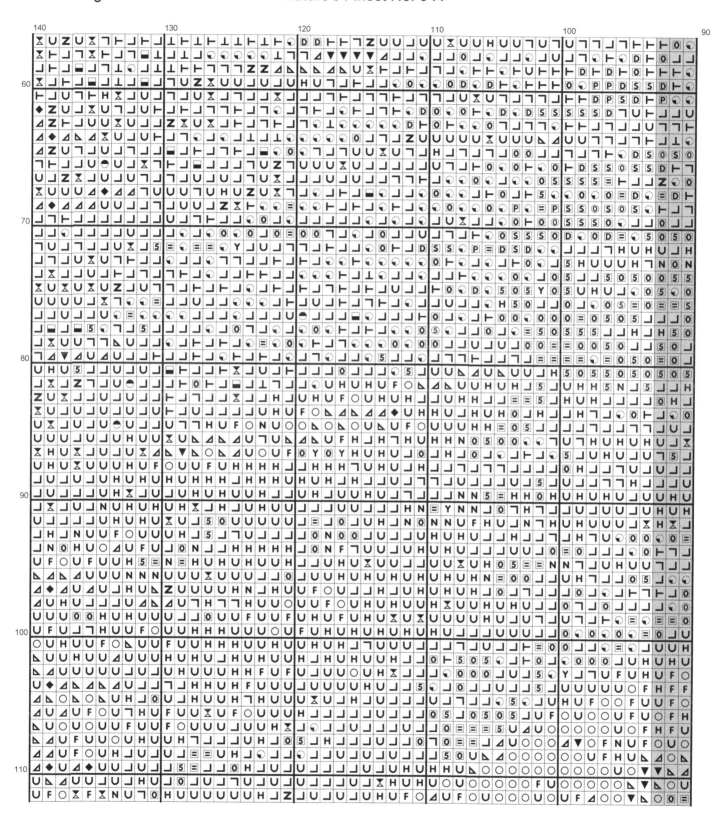

Chart Page Number 20   Nature's Finest No. 041

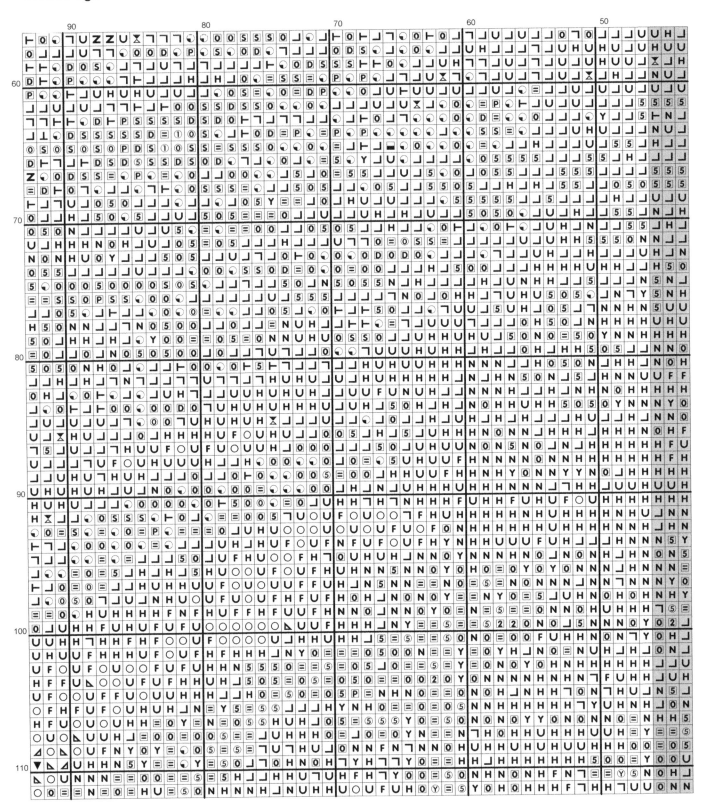

Chart Page Number 21 — Nature's Finest No. 041

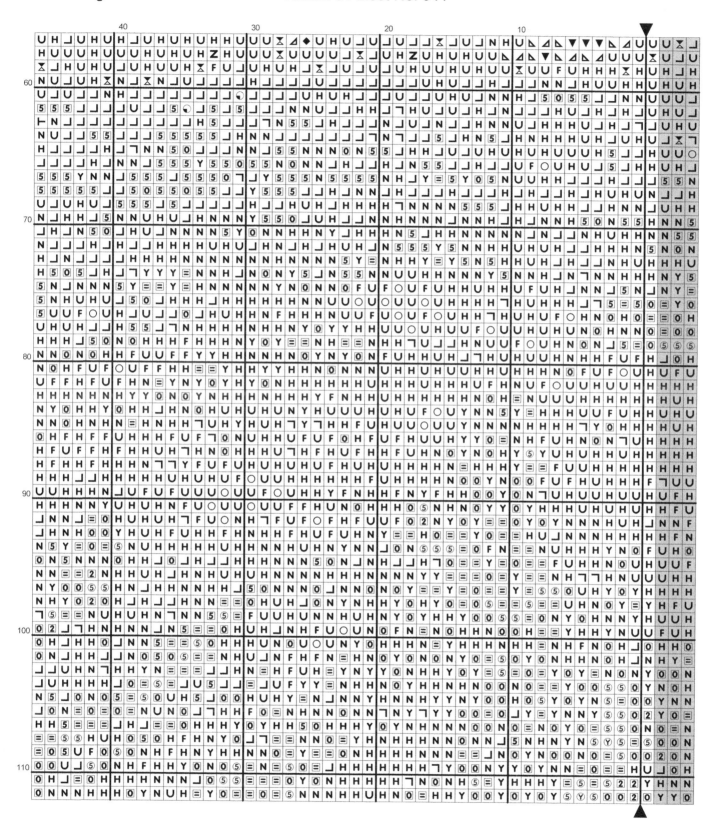

Chart Page Number 22 Nature's Finest No. 041

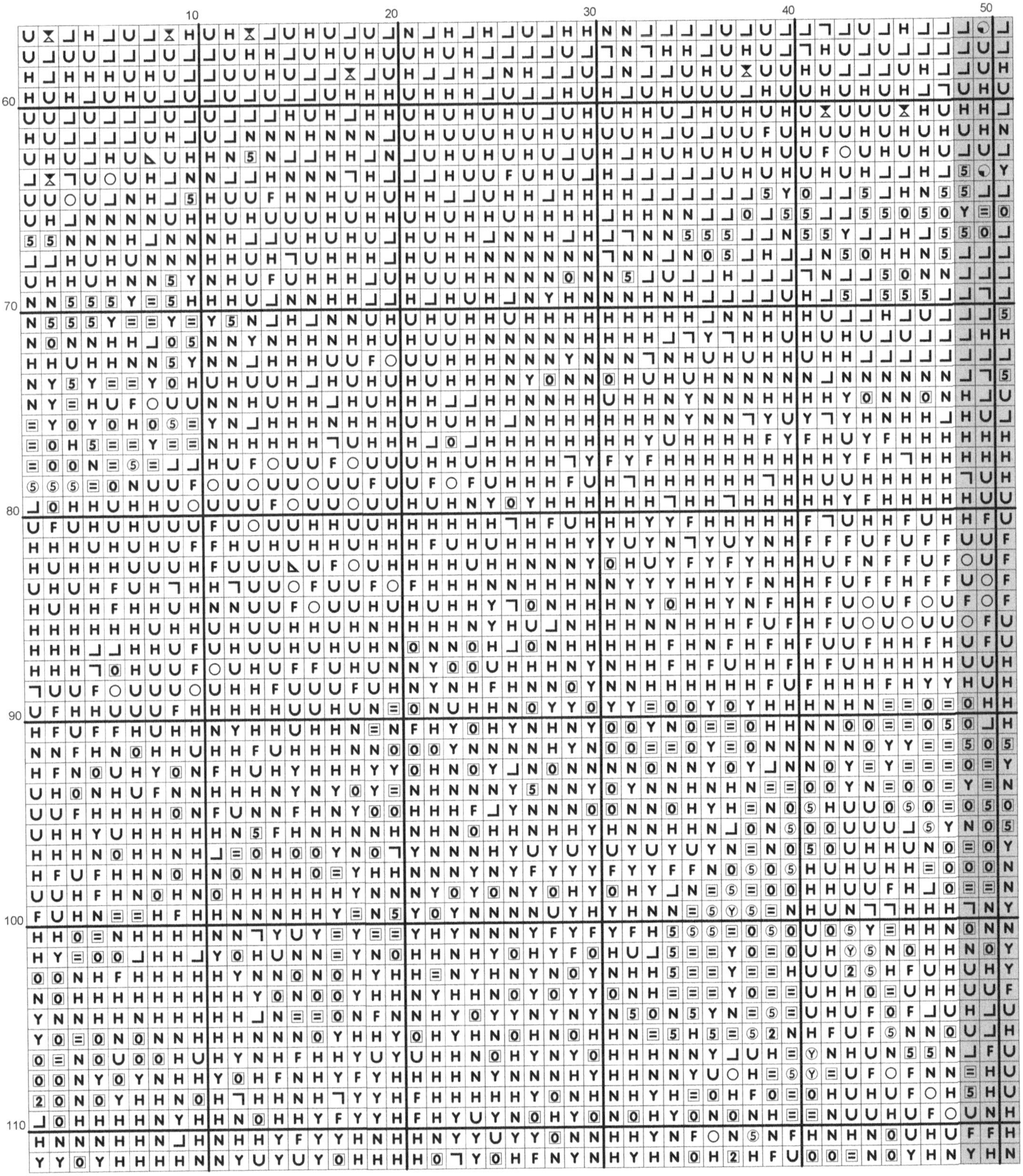

Chart Page Number 23 Nature's Finest No. 041

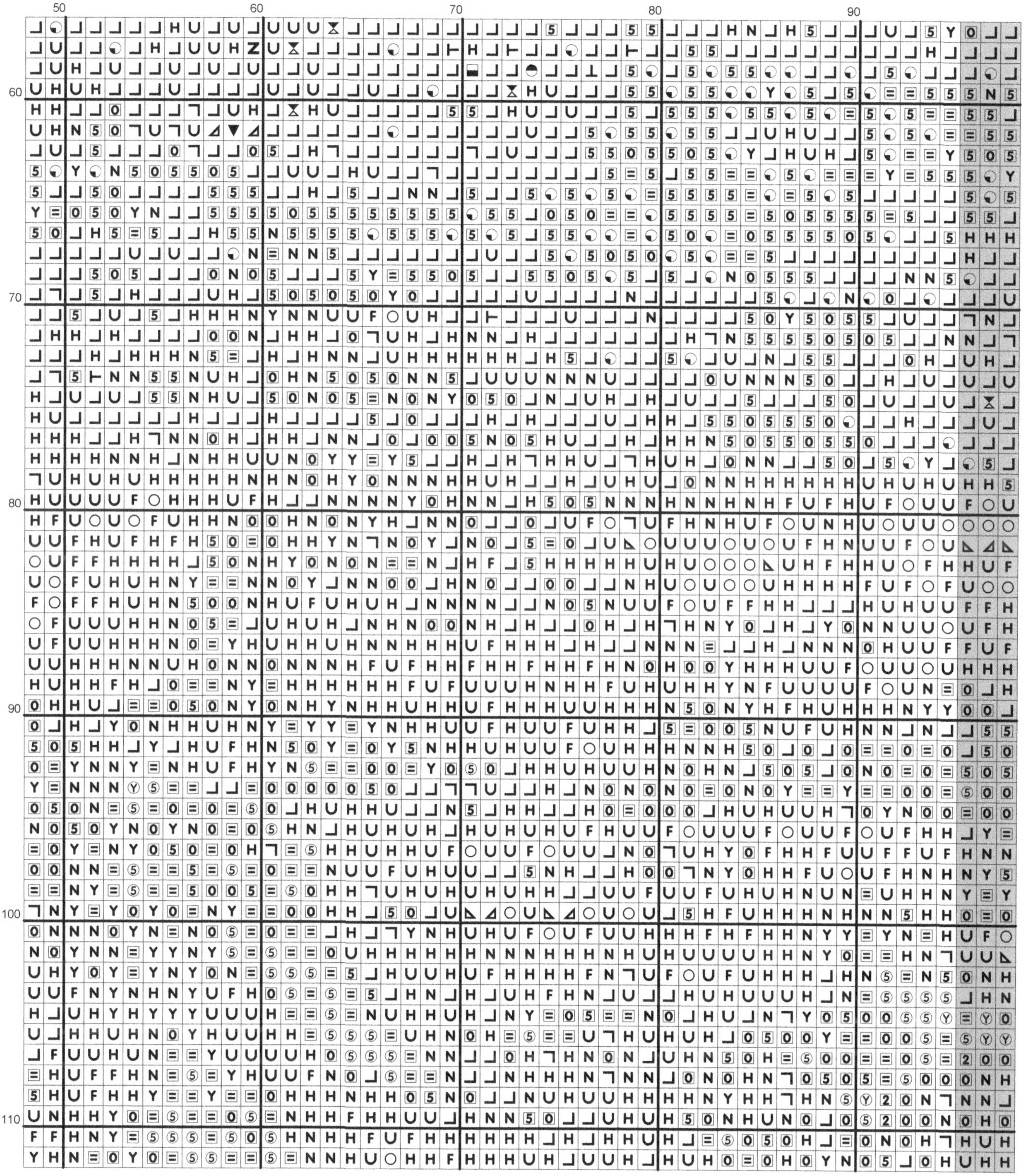

Chart Page Number 24   Nature's Finest No. 041

DMC FLOSS KEY

Stitch Count: 280 x 224
Size (when stitched on 14ct): 20.00 x 16.00 inches

Sym	No.	Color Name	Sym	No.	Color Name
6	157	Light cornflower blue	F	162	Very light blue
◇	311	Dark polar blue	5	322	Delft blue
1	334	Pale indigo blue	0	341	Hydrangea blue
▬	517	Dark wedgewood blue	D	518	Light wedgewood blue
S	597	Iceland blue	X	762	Pearl grey
N	775	Summer rain blue	7	794	Baby blue
\	798	Cobalt blue	=	799	Horizon blue
5	800	Sky blue	◡	807	Pond blue
D	809	Gentle blue	1	813	Light blue
∩	825	Sea blue	★	826	Medium sea blue
○	909	Dark Emerald Green	F	911	Golf green
2	913	Jade green	◢	924	Dark pearl green
■	939	Dark navy blue	N	943	Acid green
5	958	Seagreen	≡	959	Medium seagreen
Y	964	Light sea green	◣	991	Dark aquamarine green
0	992	Deep water green	5	993	Light green
◐	995	Carribean blue	Z	3325	Azur blue
▷	3747	Pale candy blue	L	3750	Deep petrol blue
H	3753	Moonlight blue	⊘	3755	Pastel blue
Y	3756	Cloud blue	⊥	3760	Fjord blue
D	3761	Light Sky Blue	X	3765	Dark medium blue
0	3766	Light medium blue	◆	3808	Petrol blue
Z	3809	Deep turquoise	⊢	3810	Dark turquoise
⌐	3812	Deep seagreen	U	3814	Spruce green
Z	3815	Eucalyptus Green	▼	3818	Pine tree green
P	3840	Light lavender blue	◁	3841	Igloo blue
◣	3842	Deep Wedgewood blue	◣	3847	Deep teal green
⌐	3848	Medium teal green	P	3849	Green turquoise
H	3850	Emerald green	Y	3851	Bright green
8	3865	Winter white	∅	B5200	Bright white

Shopping List

DMC Color		Qty	DMC Color		Qty	DMC Color		Qty
157	Light cornflower blue	1	992	Deep water green	1			
162	Very light blue	1	993	Light green	1			
311	Dark polar blue	1	995	Carribean blue	4			
322	Delft blue	1	3325	Azur blue	1			
334	Pale indigo blue	1	3747	Pale candy blue	1			
341	Hydrangea blue	1	3750	Deep petrol blue	1			
517	Dark wedgewood blu	1	3753	Moonlight blue	1			
518	Light wedgewood blu	1	3755	Pastel blue	1			
597	Iceland blue	1	3756	Cloud blue	2			
762	Pearl grey	1	3760	Fjord blue	1			
775	Summer rain blue	2	3761	Light Sky Blue	1			
794	Baby blue	1	3765	Dark medium blue	1			
798	Cobalt blue	1	3766	Light medium blue	1			
799	Horizon blue	2	3808	Petrol blue	1			
800	Sky blue	1	3809	Deep turquoise	1			
807	Pond blue	1	3810	Dark turquoise	1			
809	Gentle blue	1	3812	Deep seagreen	3			
813	Light blue	1	3814	Spruce green	2			
825	Sea blue	1	3815	Eucalyptus Green	1			
826	Medium sea blue	2	3818	Pine tree green	1			
909	Dark Emerald Green	1	3840	Light lavender blue	2			
911	Golf green	1	3841	Igloo blue	1			
913	Jade green	1	3842	Deep Wedgewood blu	3			
924	Dark pearl green	1	3847	Deep teal green	1			
939	Dark navy blue	1	3848	Medium teal green	1			
943	Acid green	1	3849	Green turquoise	1			
958	Seagreen	1	3850	Emerald green	2			
959	Medium seagreen	1	3851	Bright green	1			
964	Light sea green	1	3865	Winter white	1			
991	Dark aquamarine gre	1	B5200	Bright white	1			

www.stitchx.com

Nature's Finest Cross Stitch Pattern

Stitch Count: 280 x 224
Finished Size on 14ct Aida: 20" x 16"

www.stitchx.com

Chart Page Number 1 Nature's Finest No. 042

Chart Page Number 2 Nature's Finest No. 042

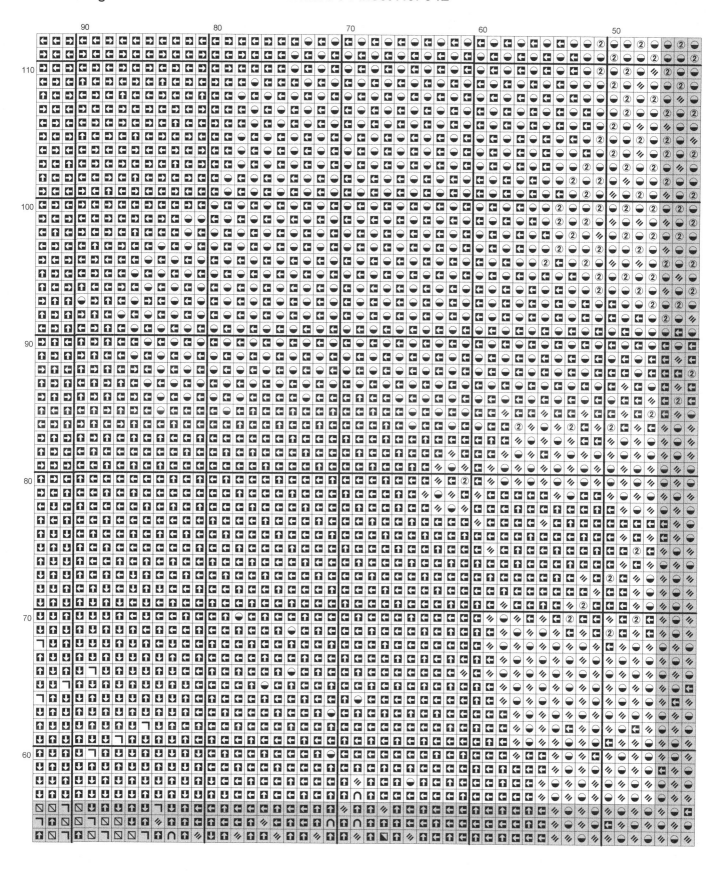

Chart Page Number 3

Nature's Finest No. 042

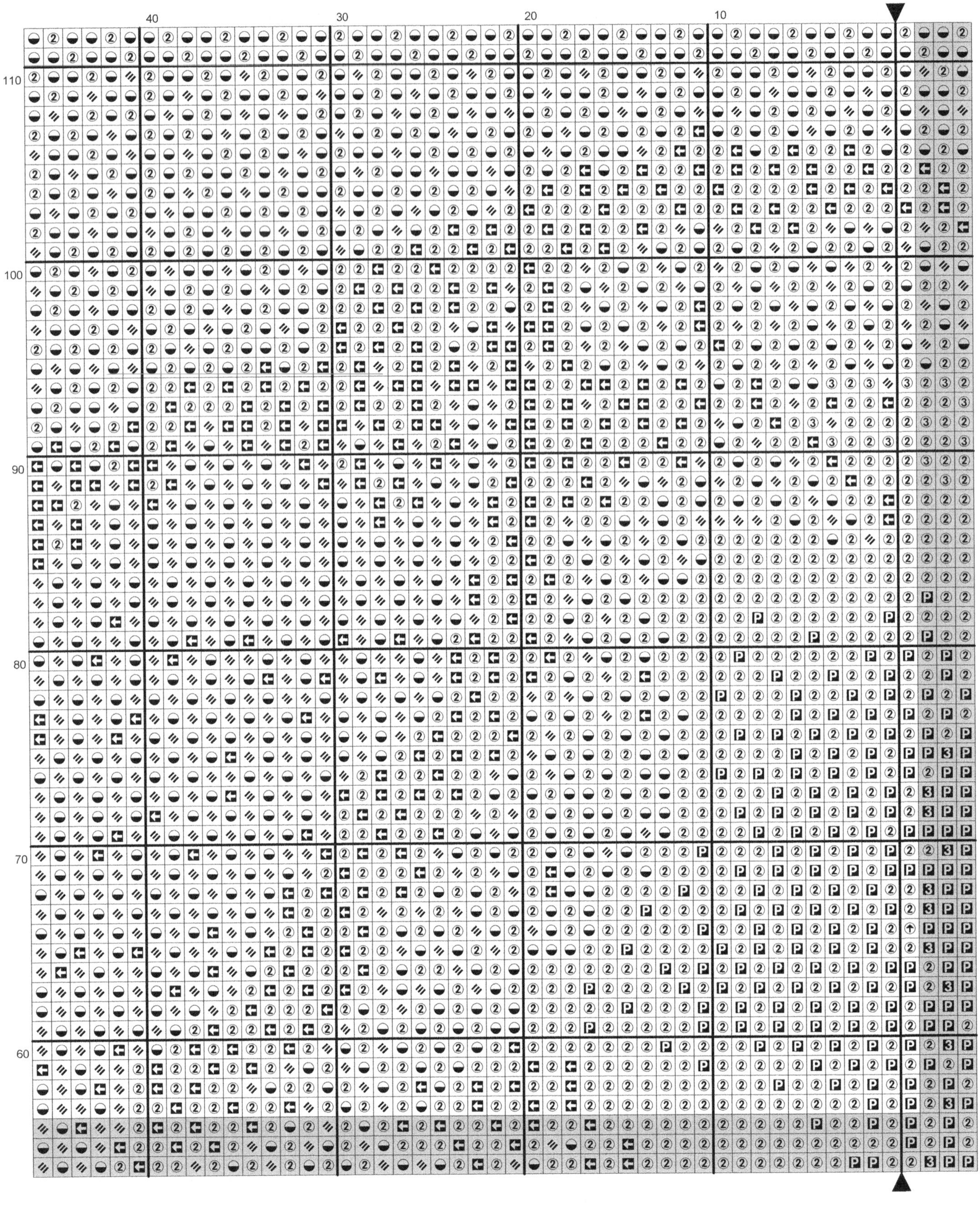

Chart Page Number 4

Nature's Finest No. 042

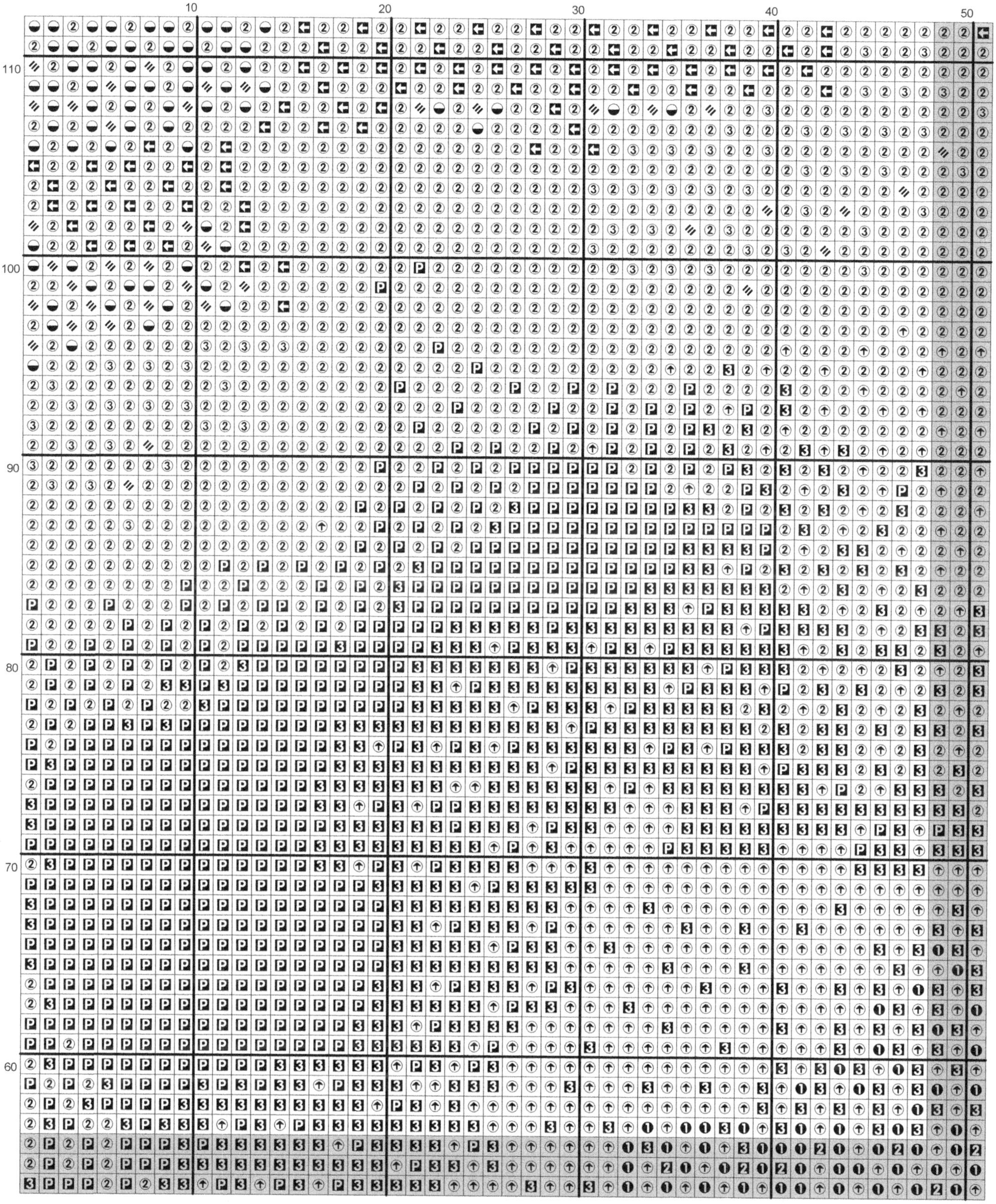

Chart Page Number 5   Nature's Finest No. 042

Chart Page Number 6 Nature's Finest No. 042

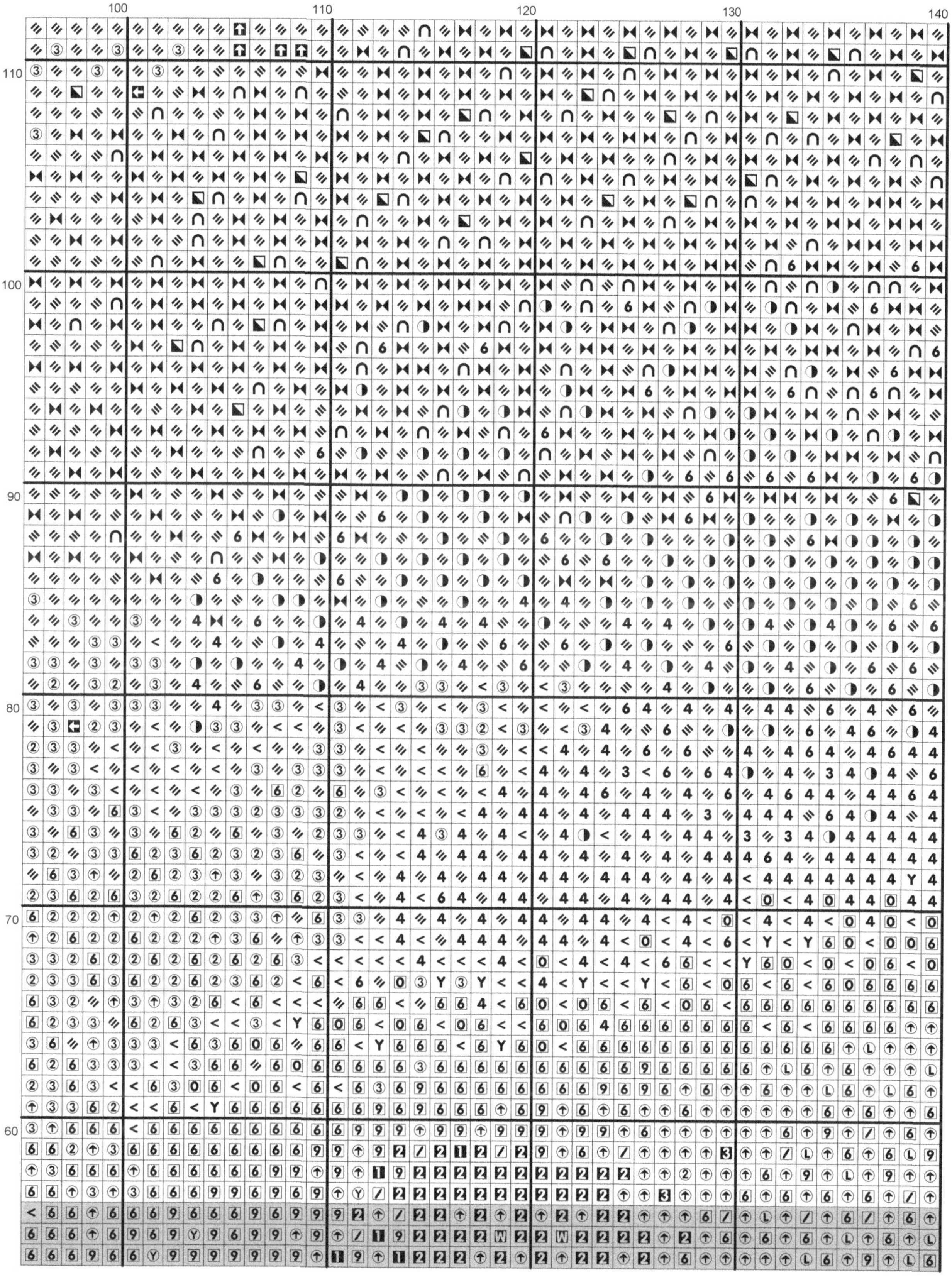

Chart Page Number 7   Nature's Finest No. 042

Chart Page Number 8   Nature's Finest No. 042

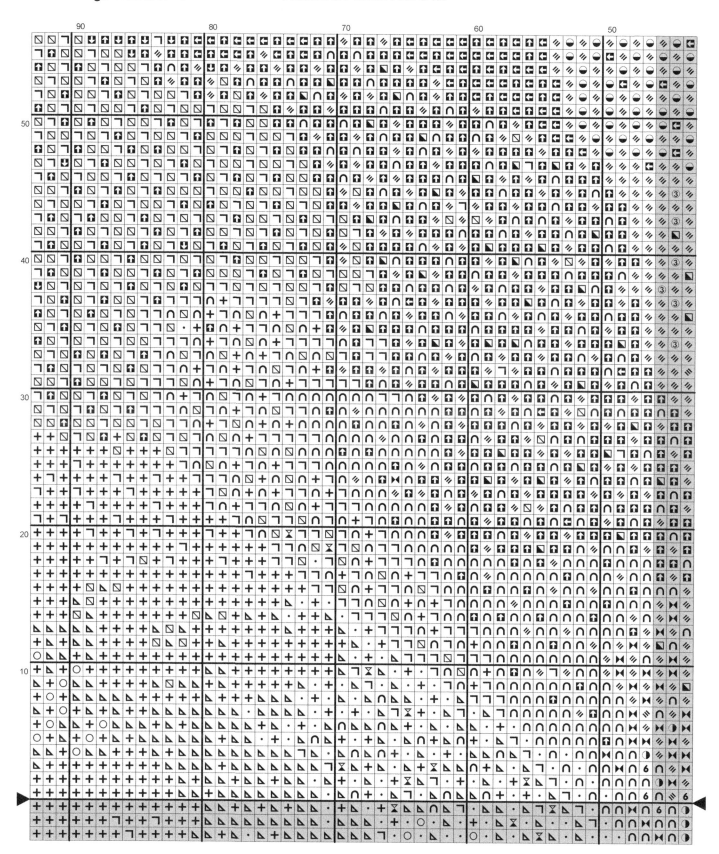

Chart Page Number 9 — Nature's Finest No. 042

Chart Page Number 10   Nature's Finest No. 042

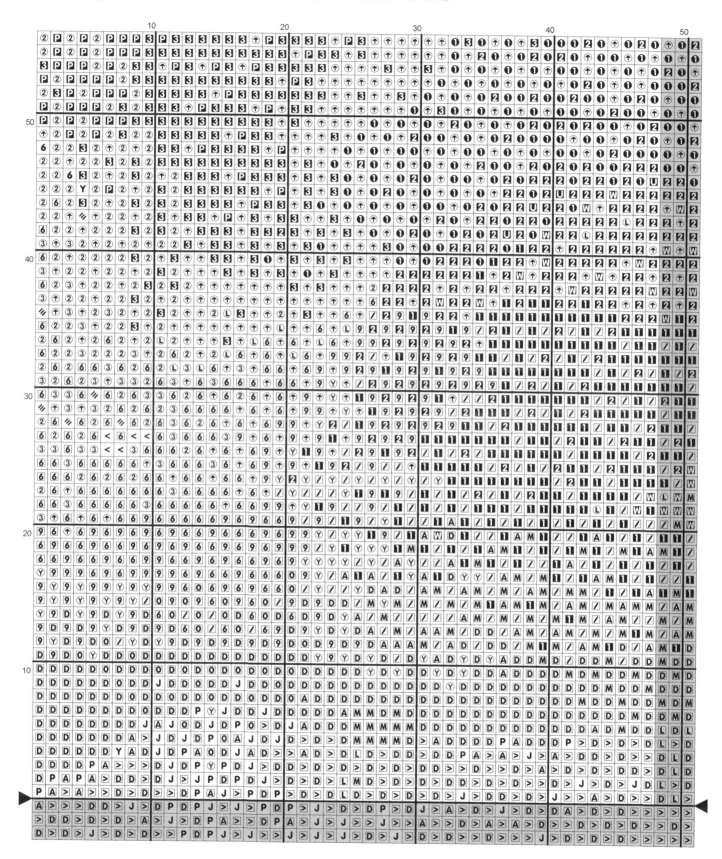

Chart Page Number 11   Nature's Finest No. 042

Chart Page Number 12   Nature's Finest No. 042

Chart Page Number 13 Nature's Finest No. 042

Chart Page Number 14 Nature's Finest No. 042

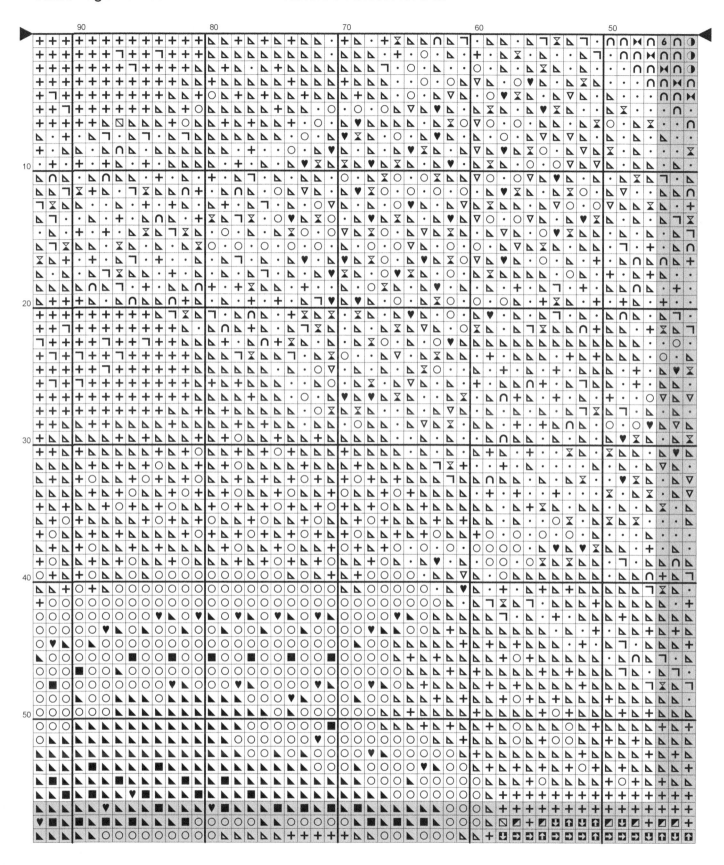

Chart Page Number 15 Nature's Finest No. 042

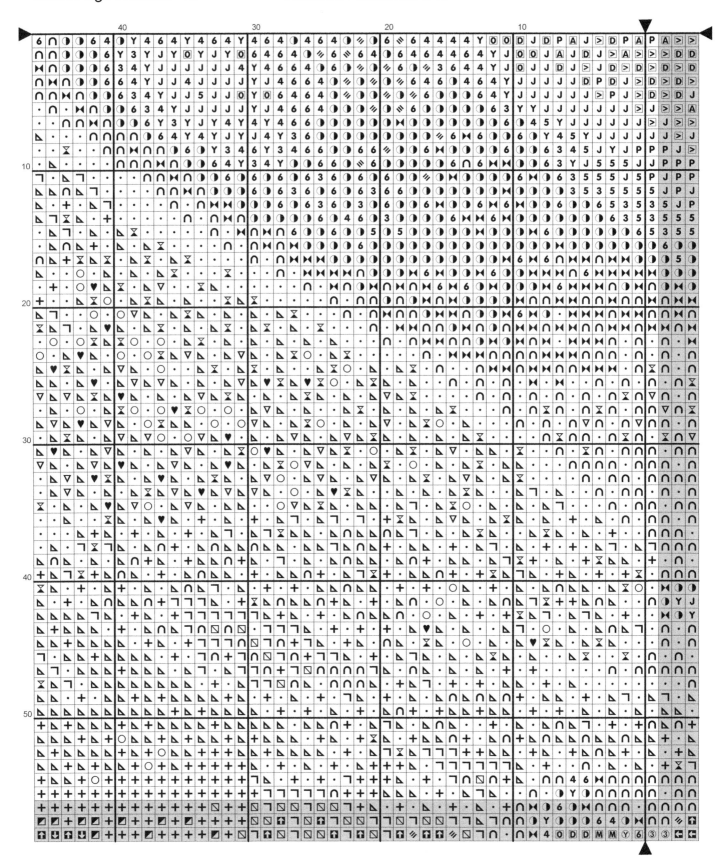

Chart Page Number 16　　　Nature's Finest No. 042

Chart Page Number 17   Nature's Finest No. 042

Chart Page Number 18 Nature's Finest No. 042

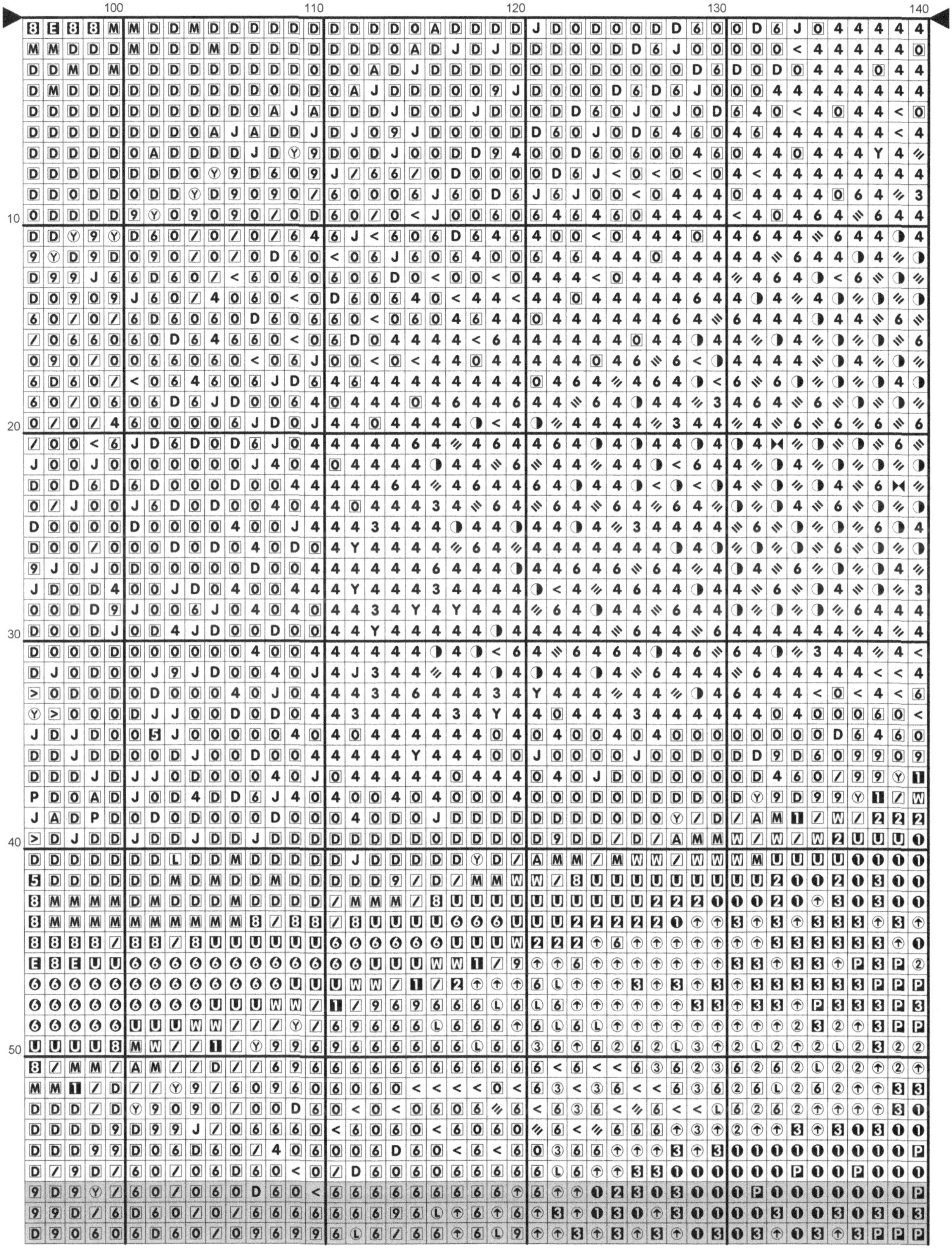

Chart Page Number 19   Nature's Finest No. 042

Chart Page Number 20   Nature's Finest No. 042

Chart Page Number 21 — Nature's Finest No. 042

Chart Page Number 22   Nature's Finest No. 042

Chart Page Number 23 Nature's Finest No. 042

Chart Page Number 24   Nature's Finest No. 042

DMC FLOSS KEY
Stitch Count: 280 x 224
Size (when stitched on 14ct): 20.00 x 16.00 inches

Sym	No.	Color Name	Sym	No.	Color Name
⇦	155	Mauve violet	◣	158	Deep mauve
②	209	Lilac	P	210	Light violet
4	223	Medium dusty pink	<	316	Heather lilac
·	327	Dark violet	⌐	333	Deep violet
◓	340	Wisteria violet	P	351	Coral
D	352	Salmon	3	356	Medium terracotta
5	402	Pottery brown	◣	451	Shell pink grey
♥	550	Blackcurrant	⫽	553	Amethyst violet
3	554	Pastel violet	2	604	Hyacinth pink
6	677	Sand gold	L	722	Orange spice
N	727	Primrose yellow	⊙	746	Vanillla
U	754	Beige rose	/	760	Grenadine pink
○	791	Dark cornflower blue	+	792	Deep cornflower blue
◪	798	Cobalt blue	◣	820	Marine blue
╏	894	Rose pink	Y	899	Medium rose
■	939	Dark navy blue	D	3064	Cinnamon brown
5	3328	Dark salmon	>	3340	Apricot
M	3341	Peach	⬆	3608	Medium pink plum
❶	3609	Light pink plum	6	3687	Raspberry mauve
6	3688	Pink mauve	A	3706	Flamingo pink
W	3708	Azalea pink	J	3712	Blush pink
◐	3722	Rosebush pink	⋈	3726	Dark antique mauve
Ⓛ	3727	Litchee mauve	Y	3731	Dark Hydrangea pink
9	3733	Ash Hydrangea pink	⟃	3740	Dark antique violet
⇧	3746	Iris violet	N	3807	Cornflower blue
D	3822	Light straw yellow	8	3825	Mango orange
0	3833	Light strawberry	▽	3834	Grape
∩	3835	Medium grape	③	3836	Light grape
⇩	3838	Dark lavender blue	⇨	3839	Mediterranean blue
E	3855	Autumn gold	⫽	3861	Light taupe

Shopping List

DMC	Color	Qty	DMC	Color	Qty	DMC Color	Qty
155	Mauve violet	2	939	Dark navy blue	6		
158	Deep mauve	2	3064	Cinnamon brown	1		
209	Lilac	3	3328	Dark salmon	1		
210	Light violet	1	3340	Apricot	1		
223	Medium dusty pink	1	3341	Peach	1		
316	Heather lilac	1	3608	Medium pink plum	1		
327	Dark violet	1	3609	Light pink plum	1		
333	Deep violet	1	3687	Raspberry mauve	1		
340	Wisteria violet	1	3688	Pink mauve	1		
351	Coral	1	3706	Flamingo pink	1		
352	Salmon	2	3708	Azalea pink	1		
356	Medium terracotta	1	3712	Blush pink	1		
402	Pottery brown	1	3722	Rosebush pink	1		
451	Shell pink grey	1	3726	Dark antique mauve	1		
550	Blackcurrant	1	3727	Litchee mauve	1		
553	Amethyst violet	3	3731	Dark Hydrangea pink	1		
554	Pastel violet	1	3733	Ash Hydrangea pink	1		
604	Hyacinth pink	1	3740	Dark antique violet	1		
677	Sand gold	1	3746	Iris violet	2		
722	Orange spice	1	3807	Cornflower blue	1		
727	Primrose yellow	1	3822	Light straw yellow	1		
746	Vanillla	1	3825	Mango orange	1		
754	Beige rose	1	3833	Light strawberry	1		
760	Grenadine pink	1	3834	Grape	1		
791	Dark cornflower blue	1	3835	Medium grape	1		
792	Deep cornflower blue	3	3836	Light grape	1		
798	Cobalt blue	1	3838	Dark lavender blue	1		
820	Marine blue	1	3839	Mediterranean blue	1		
894	Rose pink	1	3855	Autumn gold	1		
899	Medium rose	1	3861	Light taupe	1		

www.stitchx.com

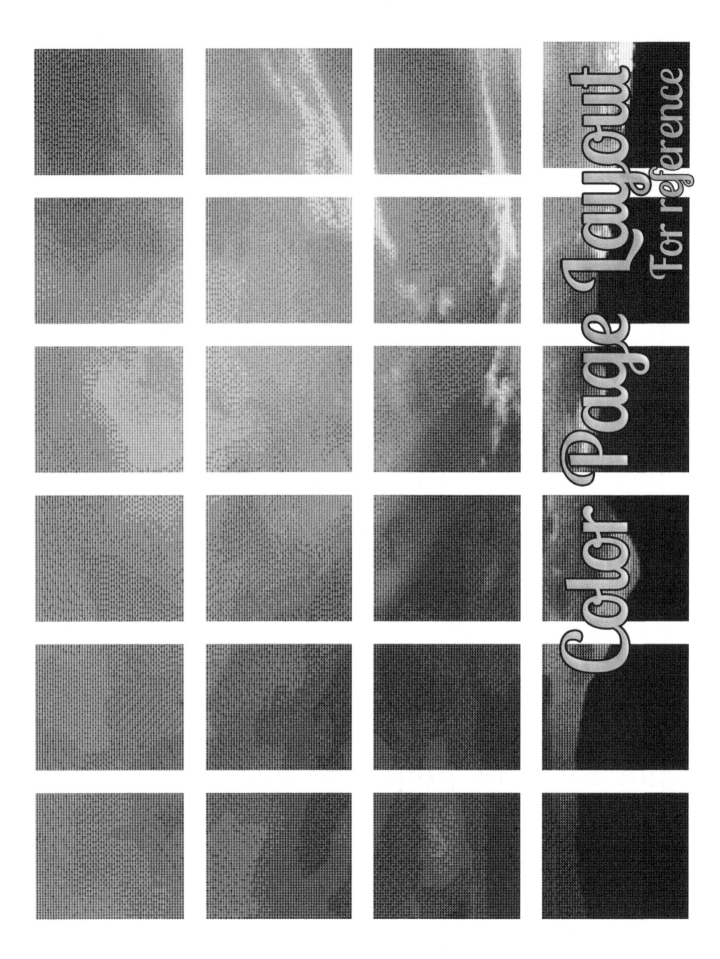

Nature's Finest Cross Stitch Pattern

Stitch Count: 280 x 224

Finished Size on 14ct Aida: 20" x 16"

www.stitchx.com

Chart Page Number 1   Nature's Finest No. 043

Chart Page Number 2 Nature's Finest No. 043

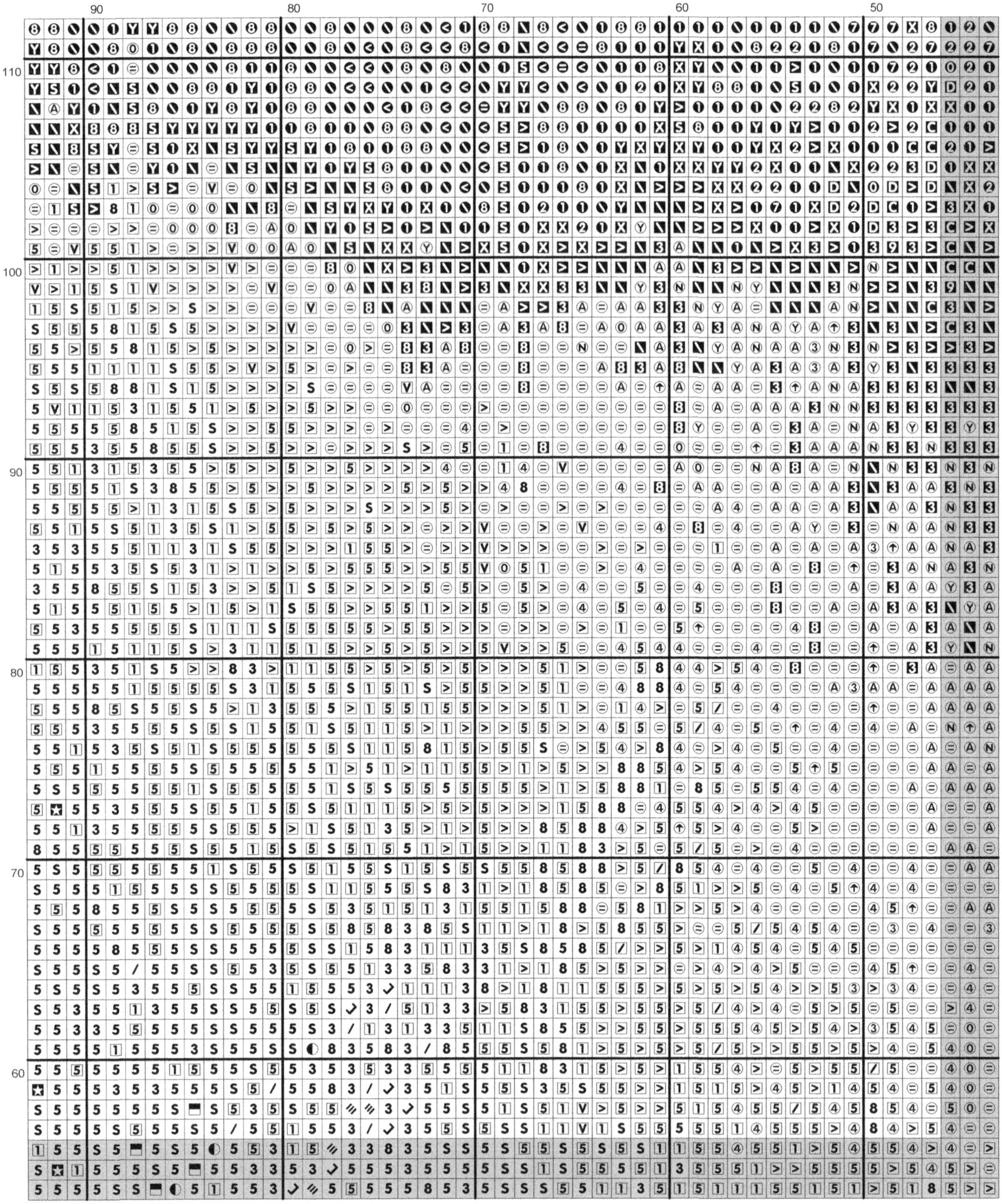

Chart Page Number 3 — Nature's Finest No. 043

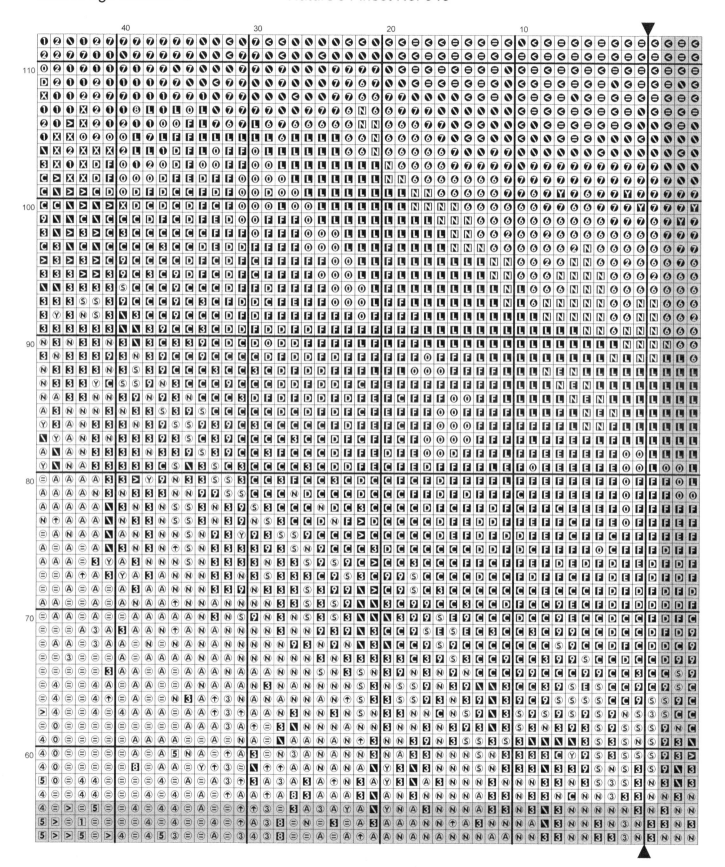

Chart Page Number 4   Nature's Finest No. 043

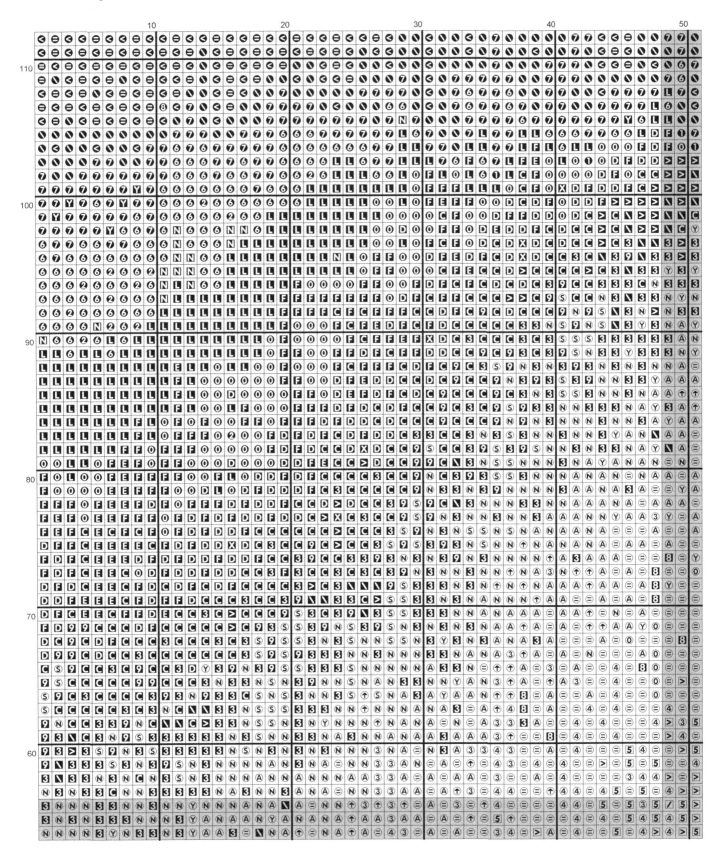

Chart Page Number 5   Nature's Finest No. 043

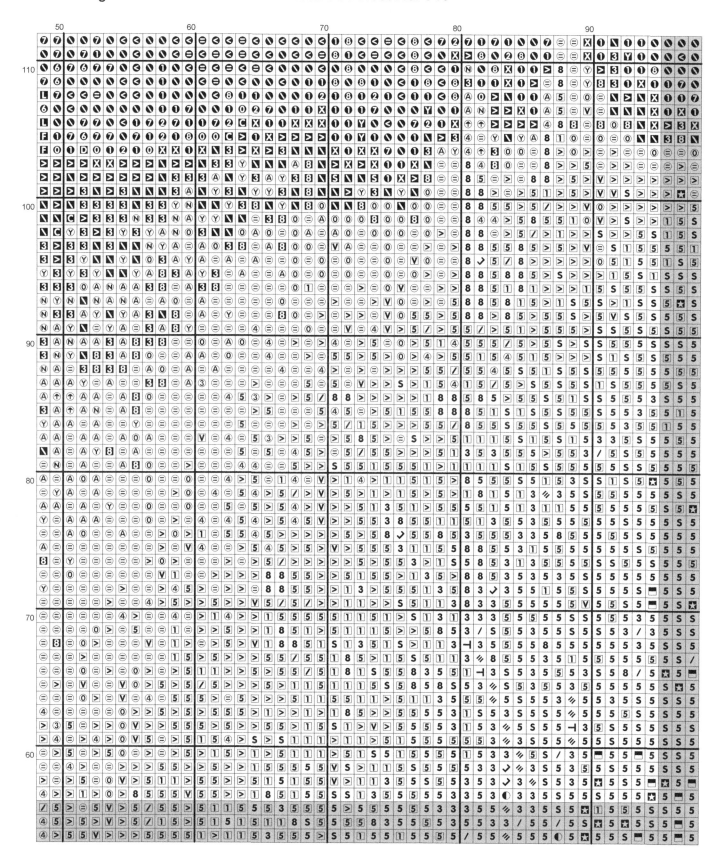

Chart Page Number 6 Nature's Finest No. 043

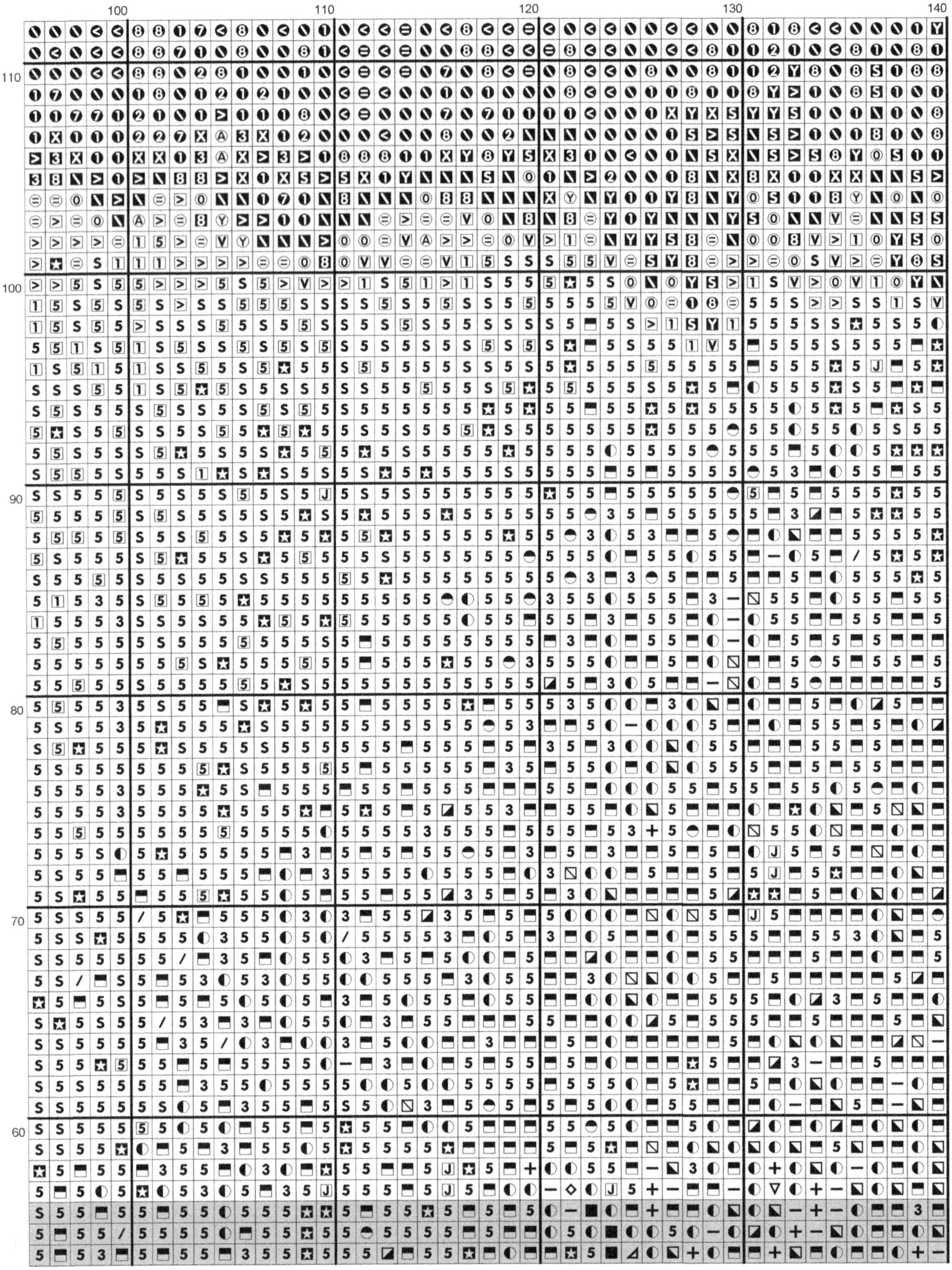

Chart Page Number 7 — Nature's Finest No. 043

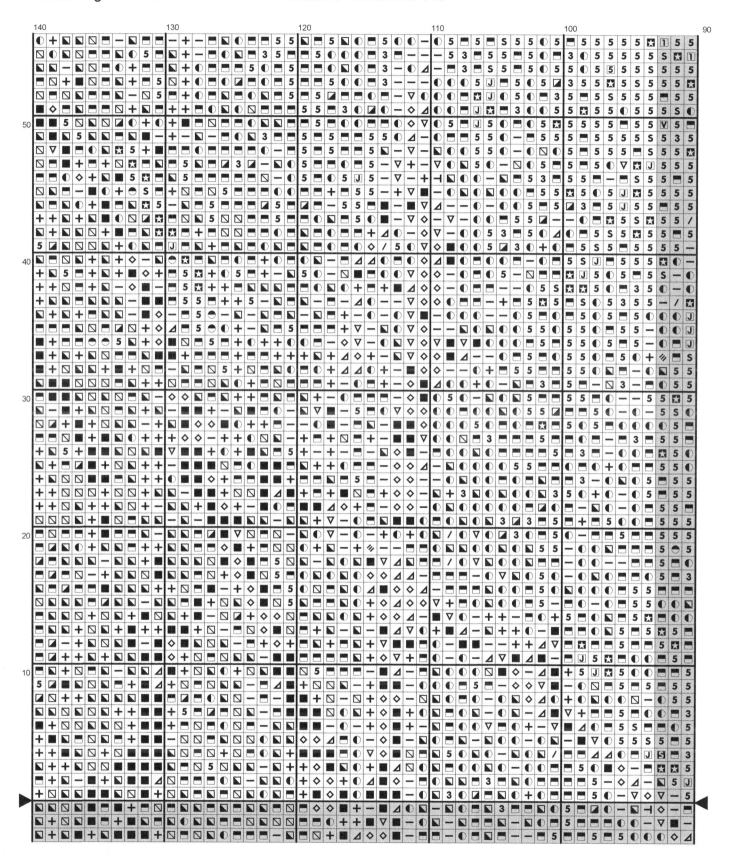

Chart Page Number 8 Nature's Finest No. 043

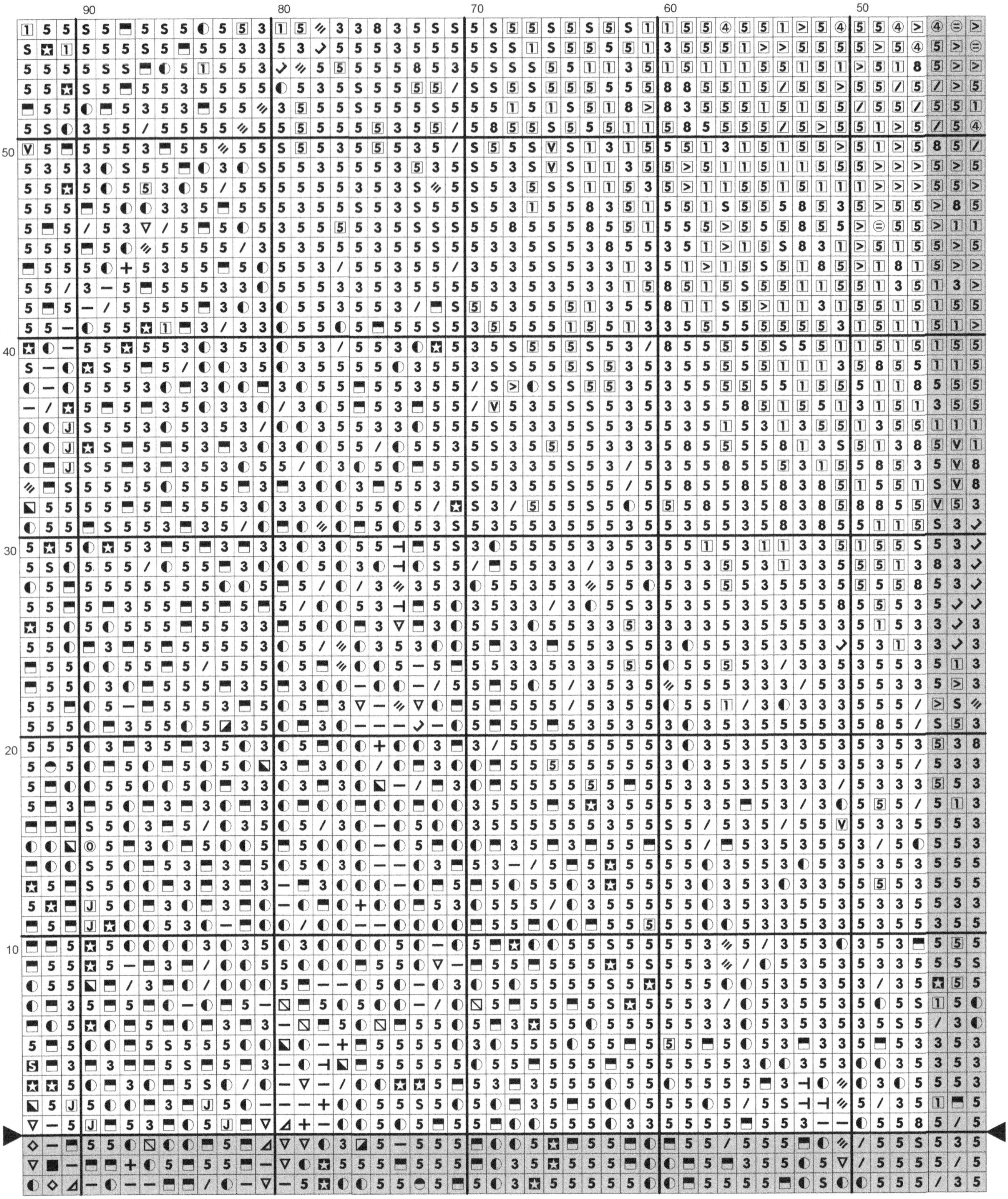

Chart Page Number 9   Nature's Finest No. 043

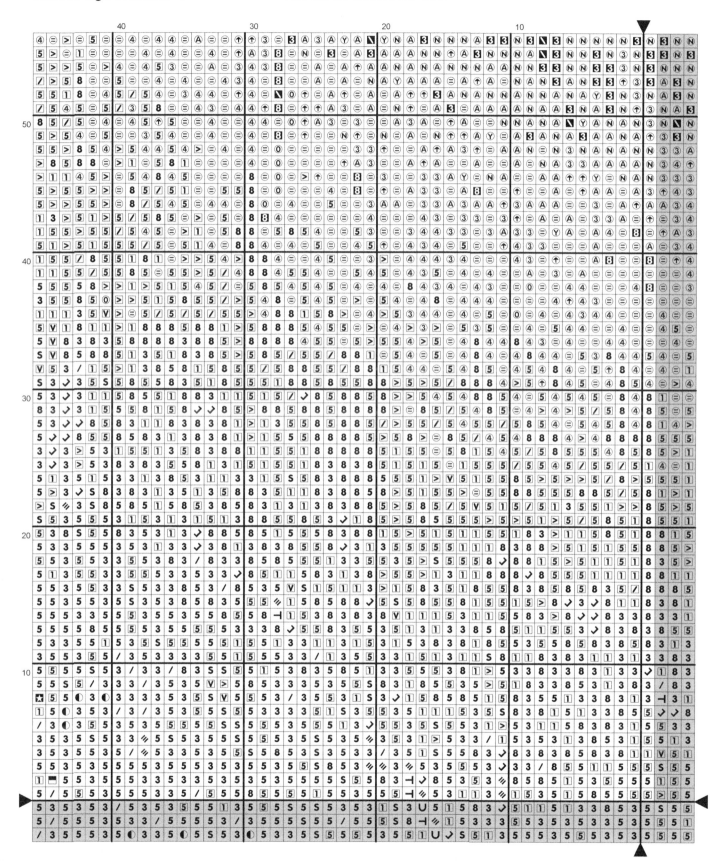

Chart Page Number 10   Nature's Finest No. 043

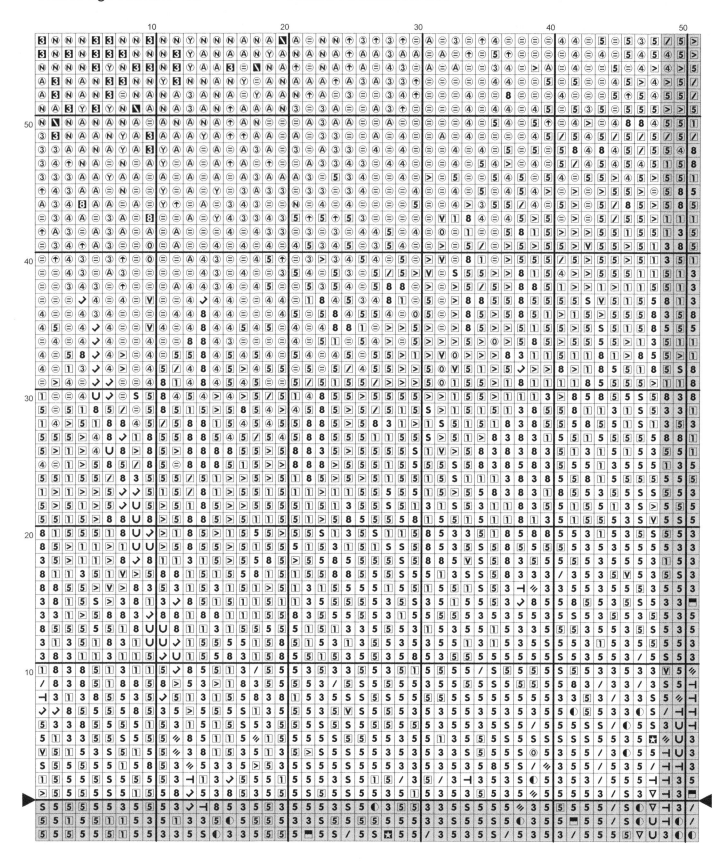

Chart Page Number 11 — Nature's Finest No. 043

Chart Page Number 12 Nature's Finest No. 043

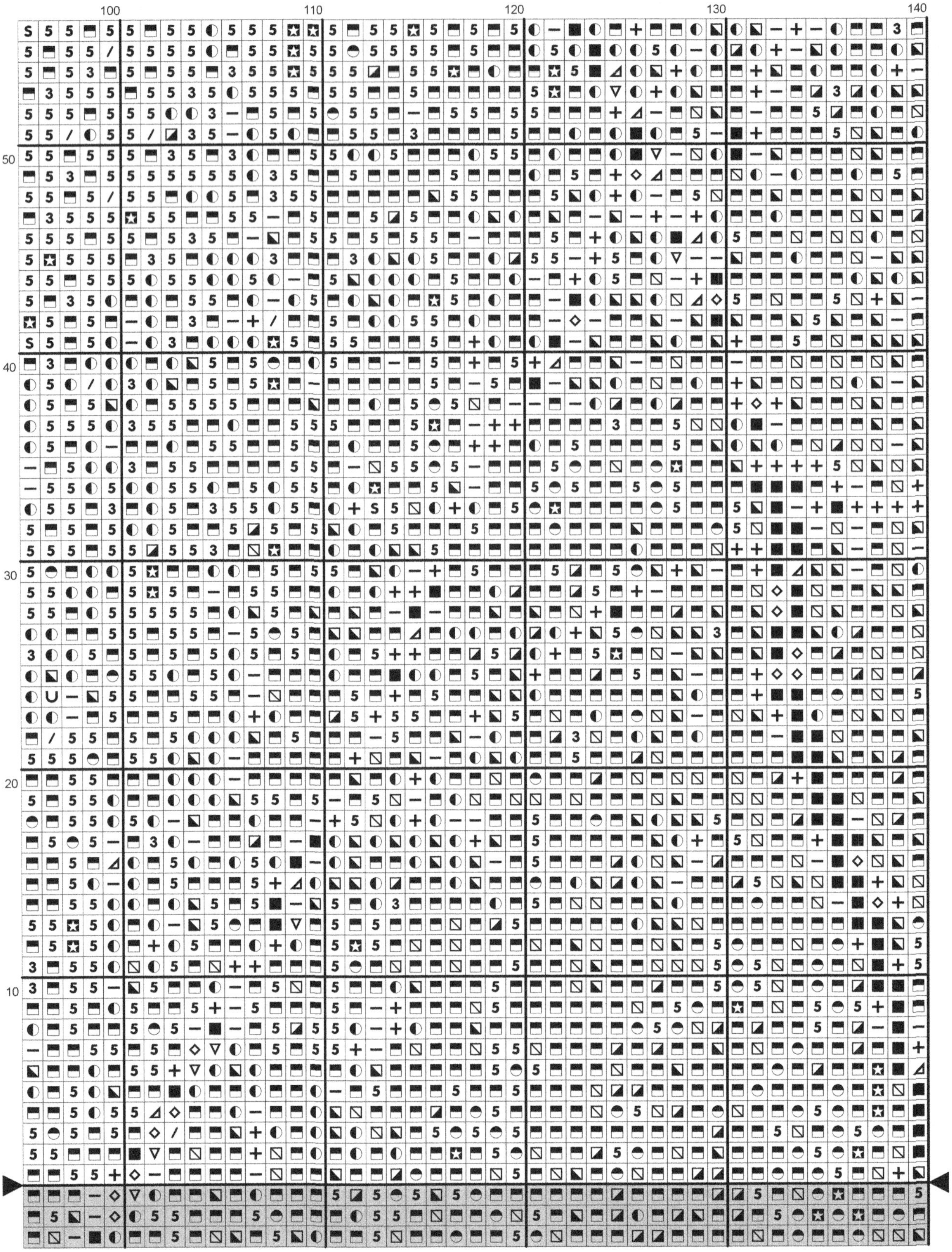

Chart Page Number 13   Nature's Finest No. 043

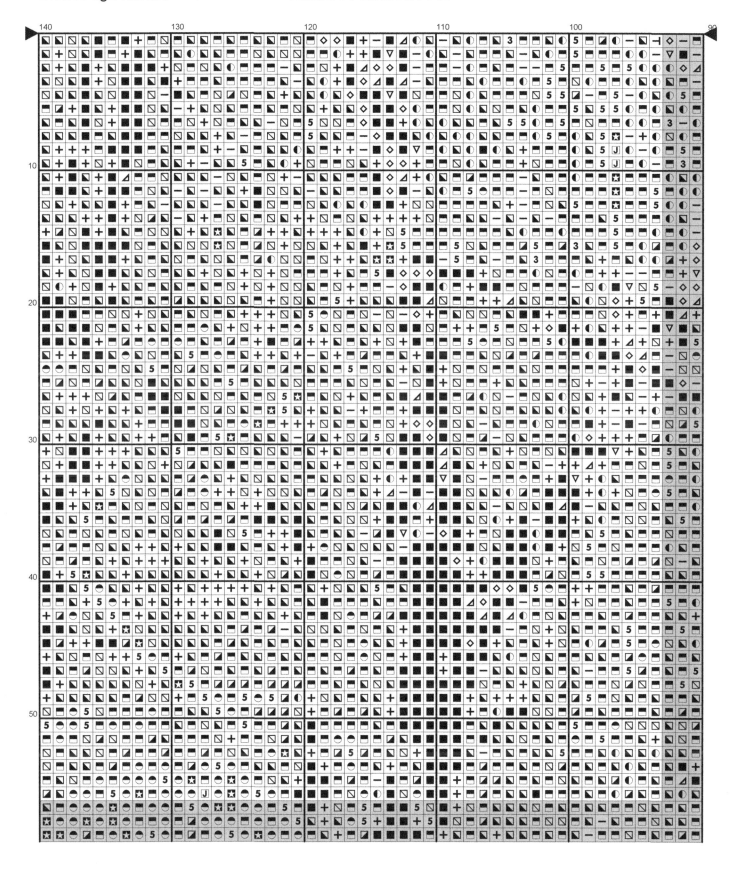

Chart Page Number 14   Nature's Finest No. 043

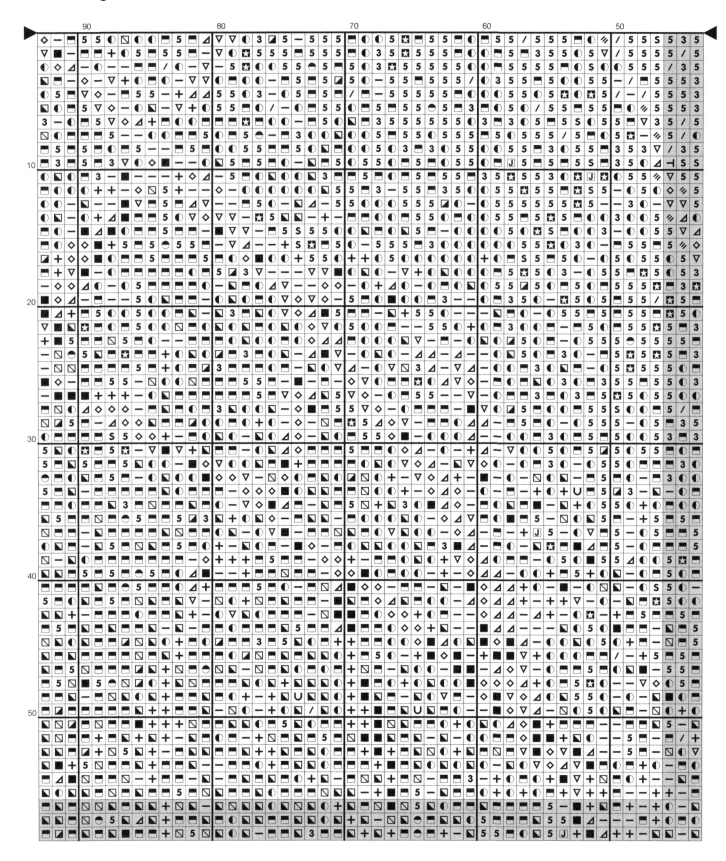

Chart Page Number 15   Nature's Finest No. 043

Chart Page Number 16   Nature's Finest No. 043

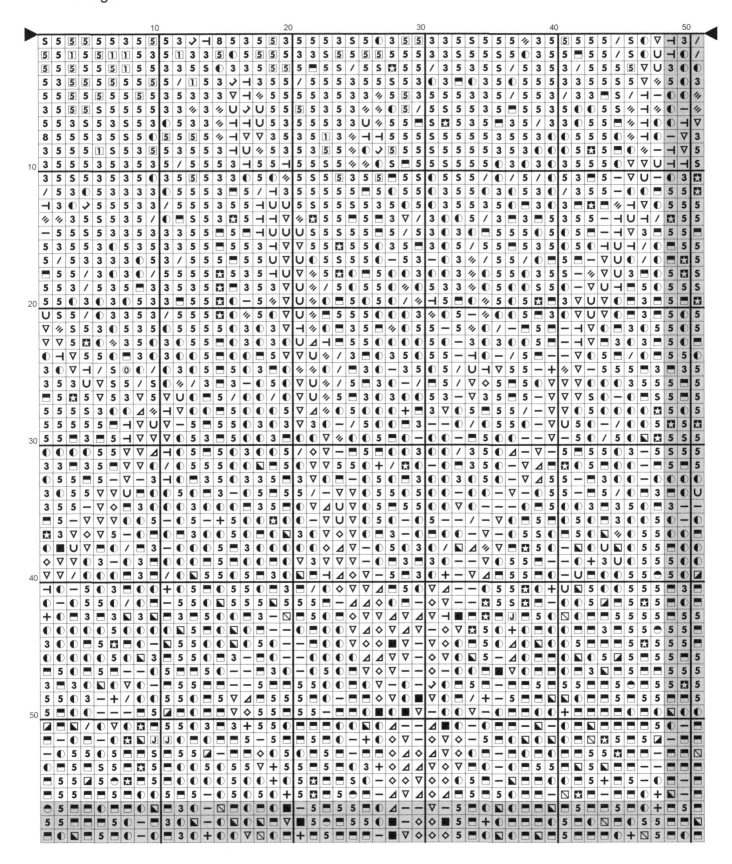

Chart Page Number 17   Nature's Finest No. 043

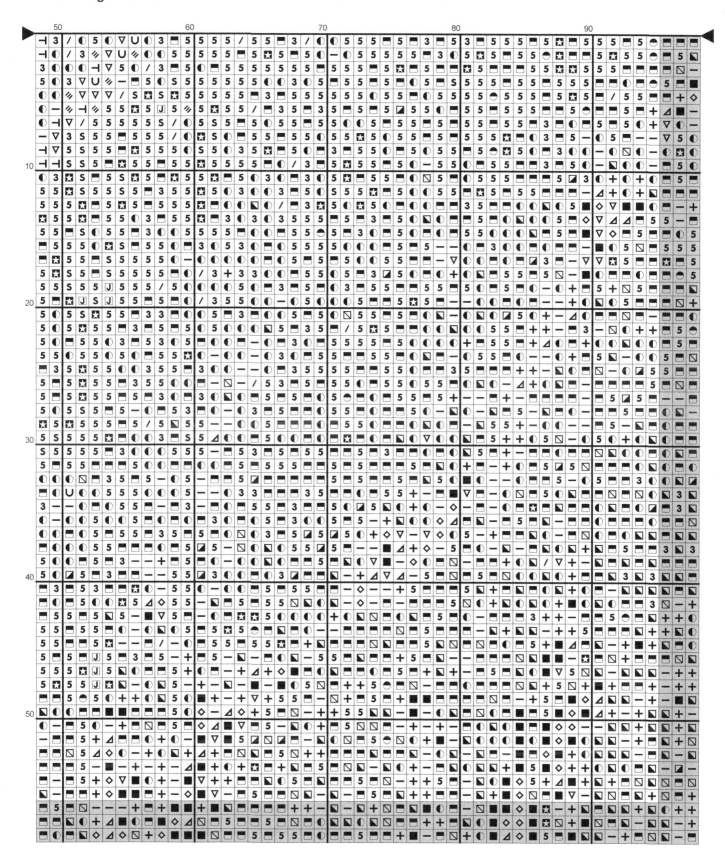

Chart Page Number 18 Nature's Finest No. 043

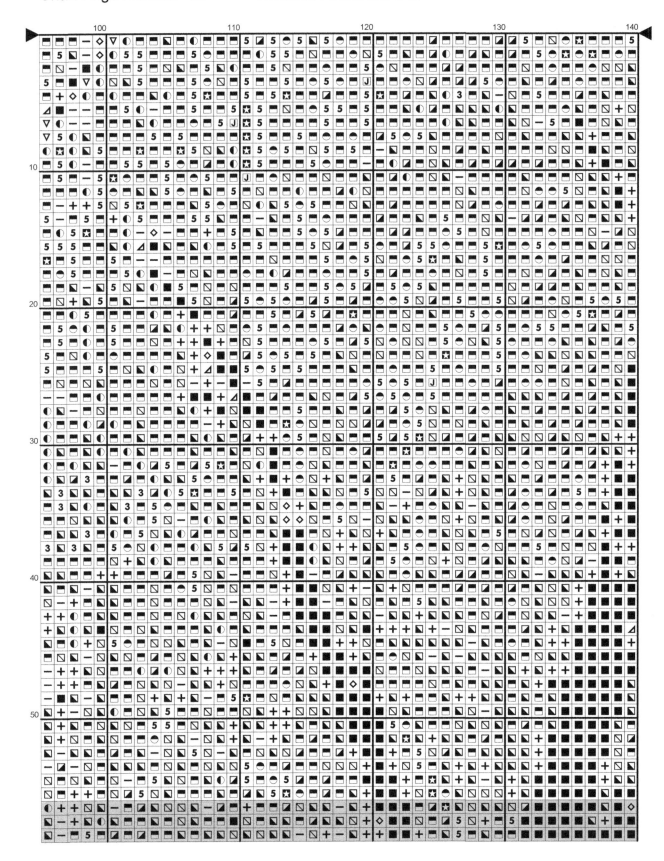

Chart Page Number 19   Nature's Finest No. 043

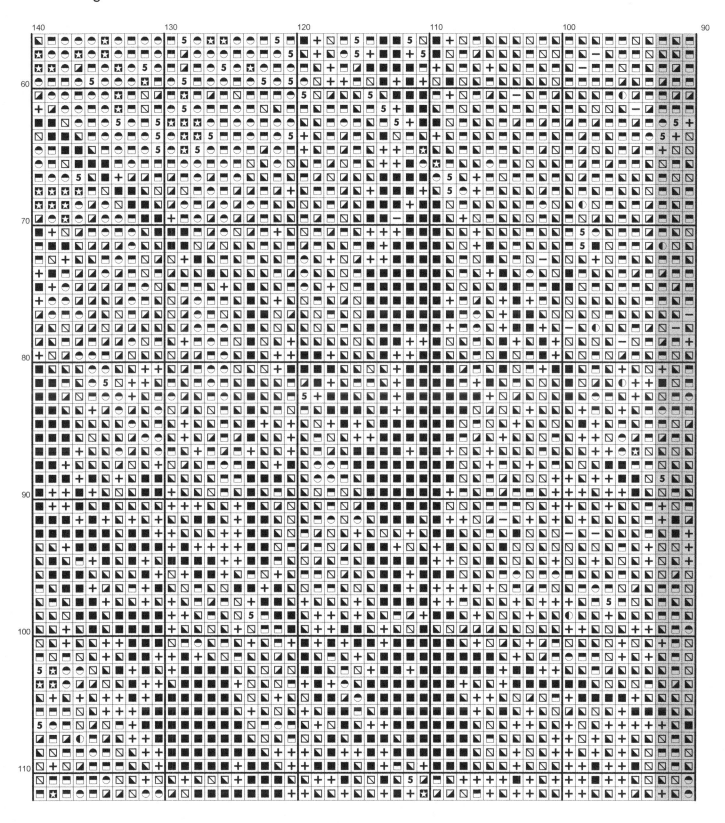

Chart Page Number 20   Nature's Finest No. 043

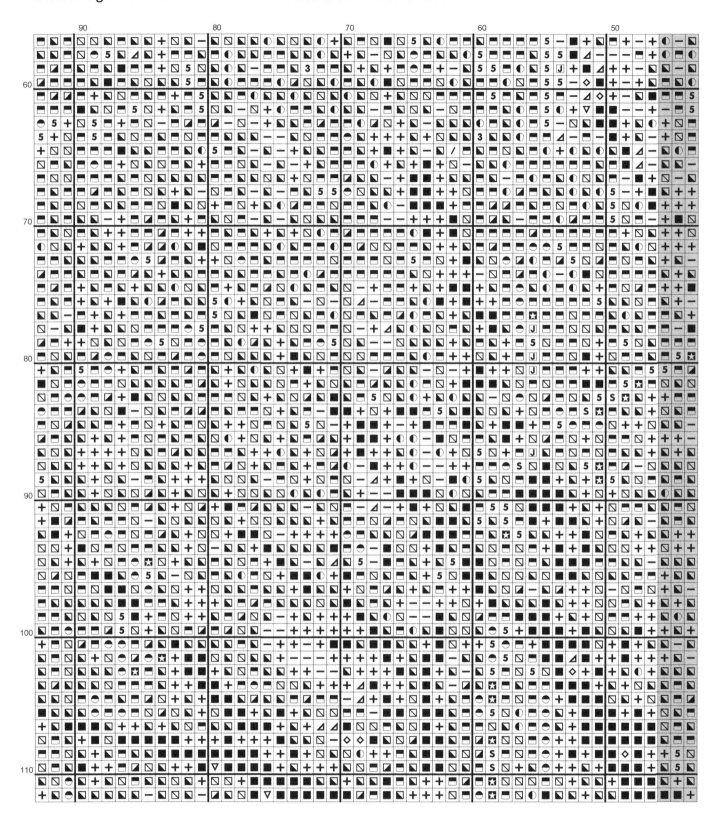

Chart Page Number 21   Nature's Finest No. 043

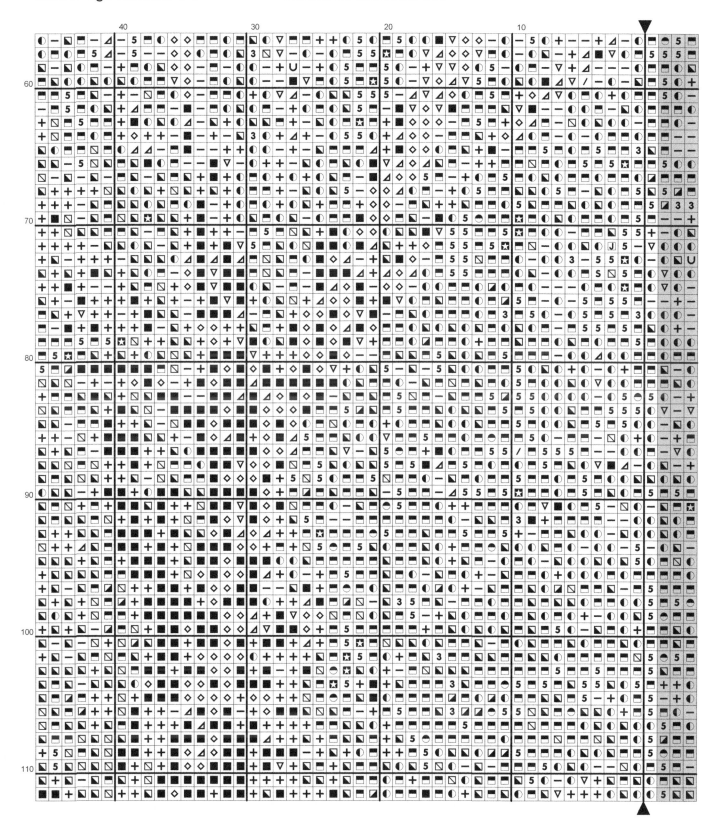

Chart Page Number 22 Nature's Finest No. 043

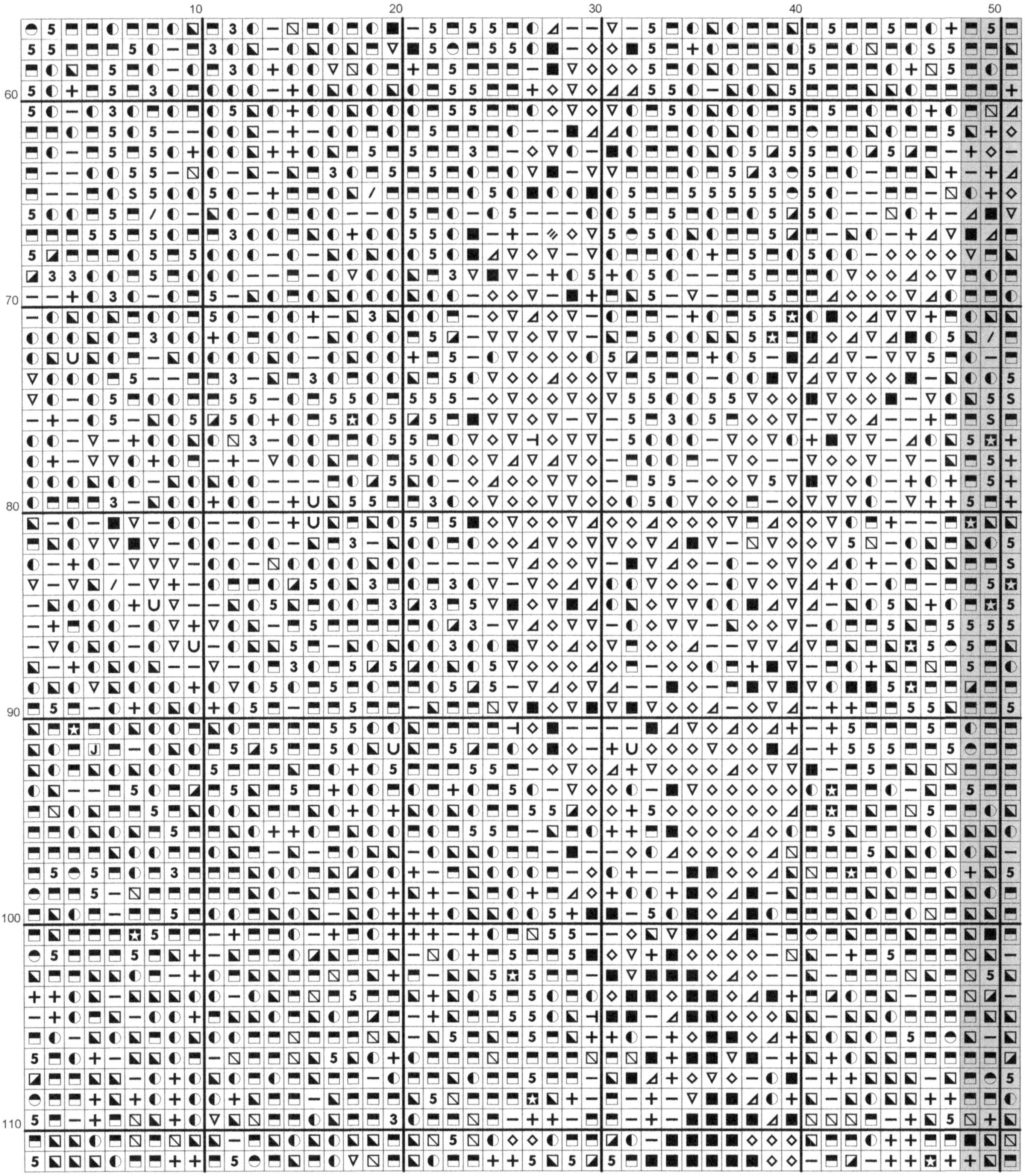

Chart Page Number 23 — Nature's Finest No. 043

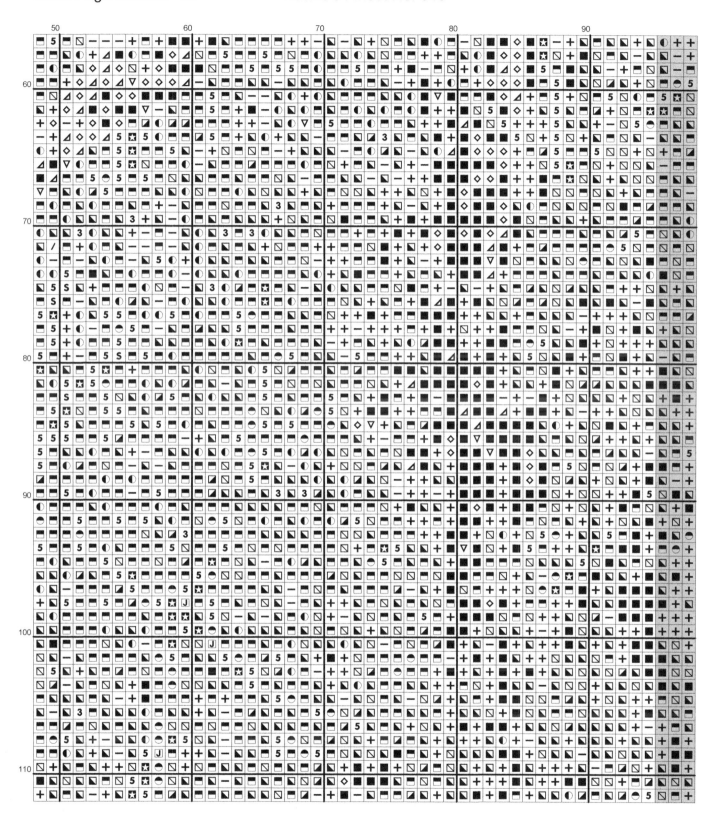

Chart Page Number 24 — Nature's Finest No. 043

DMC FLOSS KEY

Stitch Count: 280 x 224
Size (when stitched on 14ct): 20.00 x 16.00 inches

Sym	No.	Color Name	Sym	No.	Color Name
▽	154	Prune rose	★	161	Ash blue
|v|	169	Pewter grey	◇	310	Black
◐	312	Night blue	Y	316	Heather lilac
5	317	Steel grey	N	336	Indigo blue
N	407	Clay brown	◑	413	Iron grey
s	414	Lead grey	9	422	Light oak
C	437	Camel	|>|	451	Shell pink grey
/	535	Stone grey	0	543	Shell beige
/|	640	Green grey	S	644	Light green grey
|1|	646	Platinum grey	L	677	Sand gold
D	738	Sahara cream	N	744	Grapefruit yellow
◐	746	Vanillla	⌄	779	Sepia mauve
◪	803	Ink blue	+	823	Blueberry blue
④	840	Hare brown	Ⓐ	841	Deer brown
▷	842	Beige rope	■	930	Slate grey
J	931	Blue grey	U	938	Espresso brown
■	939	Dark navy blue	0	945	Eggshell cream
X	950	Beige	⫽	3021	Cliff grey
8	3023	Light platinum grey	⊣	3031	Dark Mocha brown
Y	3033	Antique silver	|5|	3041	Medium lilac
ⓞ	3042	Lilac	❷	3047	Silver birch beige
ⓢ	3064	Cinnamon brown	❻	3078	Pale yellow
◿	3371	Ebony	3	3740	Dark antique violet
⊠	3750	Deep petrol blue	③	3772	Rosy tan
N	3782	Gingerbread brown	—	3799	Anthracite grey
❼	3823	Ivory	E	3827	Beech brown
F	3856	Pale beechwood	8	3860	Taupe mauve
⊜	3861	Light taupe	⊕	3863	Otter brown
3	3864	Light mocha brown	◁	3865	Winter white
8	ECRU	ECRU	⊖	White	White

Shopping List

DMC	Color	Qty	DMC	Color	Qty	DMC Color	Qty
154	Prune rose	1	931	Blue grey	1		
161	Ash blue	1	938	Espresso brown	1		
169	Pewter grey	1	939	Dark navy blue	2		
310	Black	1	945	Eggshell cream	1		
312	Night blue	1	950	Beige	1		
316	Heather lilac	1	3021	Cliff grey	1		
317	Steel grey	6	3023	Light platinum grey	1		
336	Indigo blue	3	3031	Dark Mocha brown	1		
407	Clay brown	1	3033	Antique silver	1		
413	Iron grey	3	3041	Medium lilac	2		
414	Lead grey	1	3042	Lilac	1		
422	Light oak	1	3047	Silver birch beige	1		
437	Camel	1	3064	Cinnamon brown	1		
451	Shell pink grey	1	3078	Pale yellow	1		
535	Stone grey	1	3371	Ebony	1		
543	Shell beige	1	3740	Dark antique violet	2		
640	Green grey	1	3750	Deep petrol blue	2		
644	Light green grey	1	3772	Rosy tan	1		
646	Platinum grey	1	3782	Gingerbread brown	1		
677	Sand gold	1	3799	Anthracite grey	2		
738	Sahara cream	1	3823	Ivory	1		
744	Grapefruit yellow	1	3827	Beech brown	1		
746	Vanilla	1	3856	Pale beechwood	1		
779	Sepia mauve	1	3860	Taupe mauve	1		
803	Ink blue	1	3861	Light taupe	1		
823	Blueberry blue	2	3863	Otter brown	1		
840	Hare brown	1	3864	Light mocha brown	1		
841	Deer brown	1	3865	Winter white	1		
842	Beige rope	1	ECRU	ECRU	1		
930	Slate grey	6	White	White	1		

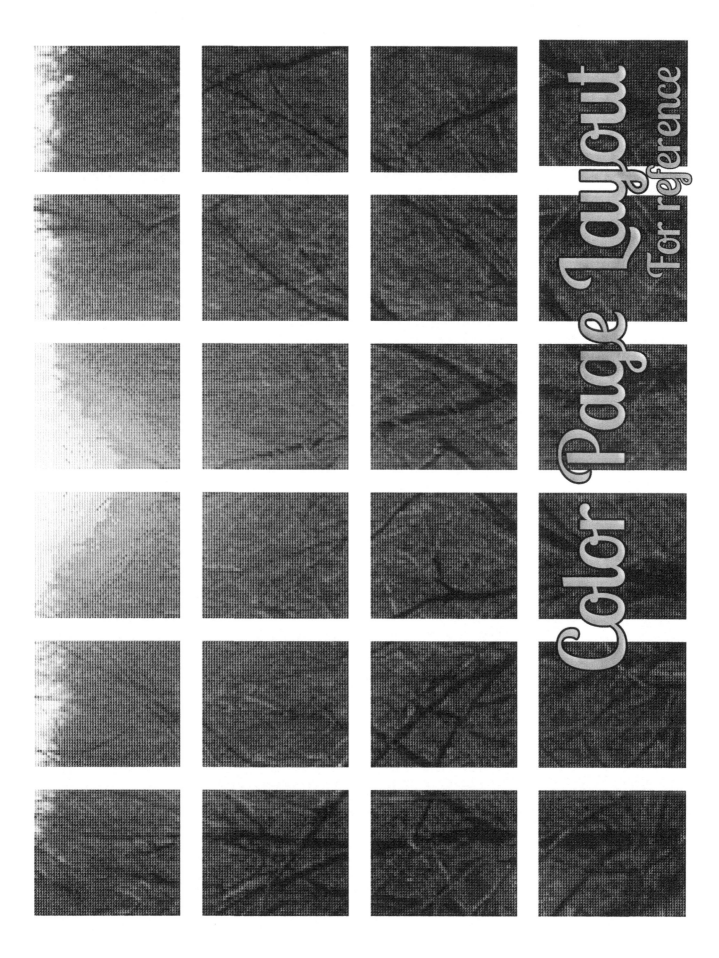

Nature's Finest Cross Stitch Pattern

Stitch Count: 280 x 224
Finished Size on 14ct Aida: 20" x 16"

www.stitchx.com

Chart Page Number 1 Nature's Finest No. 044

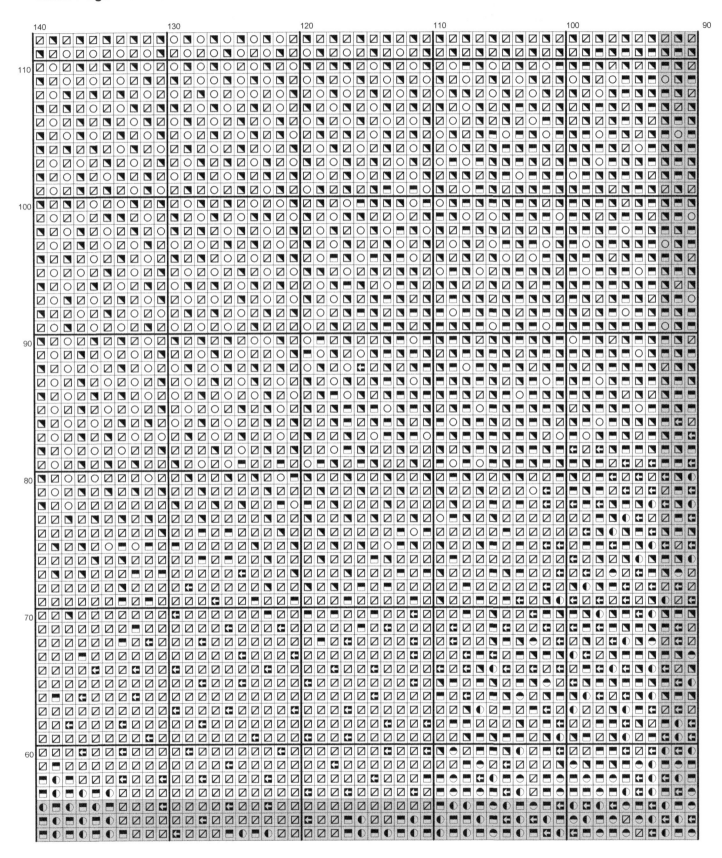

Chart Page Number 2 — Nature's Finest No. 044

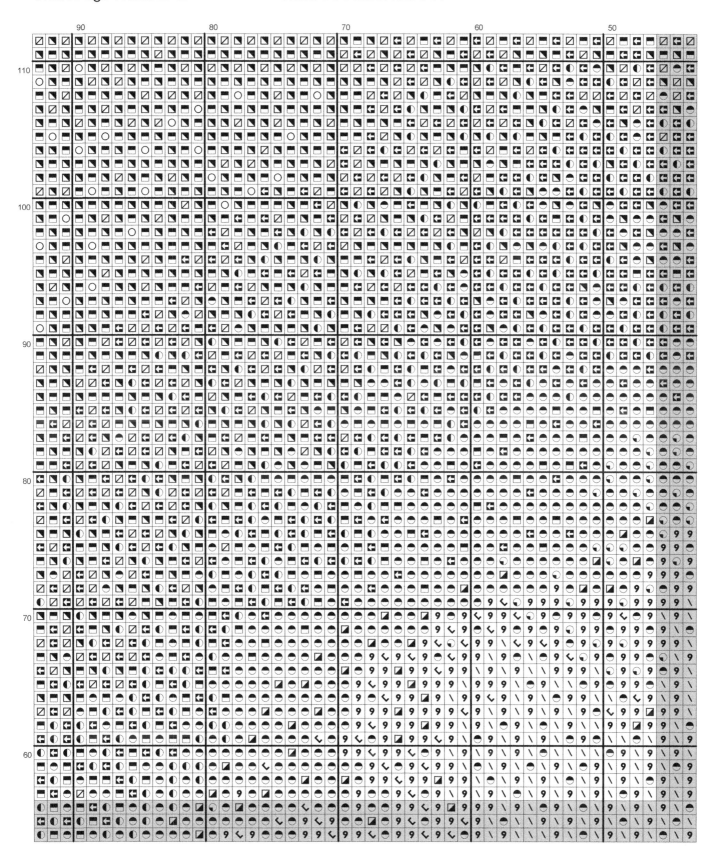

Chart Page Number 3　　Nature's Finest No. 044

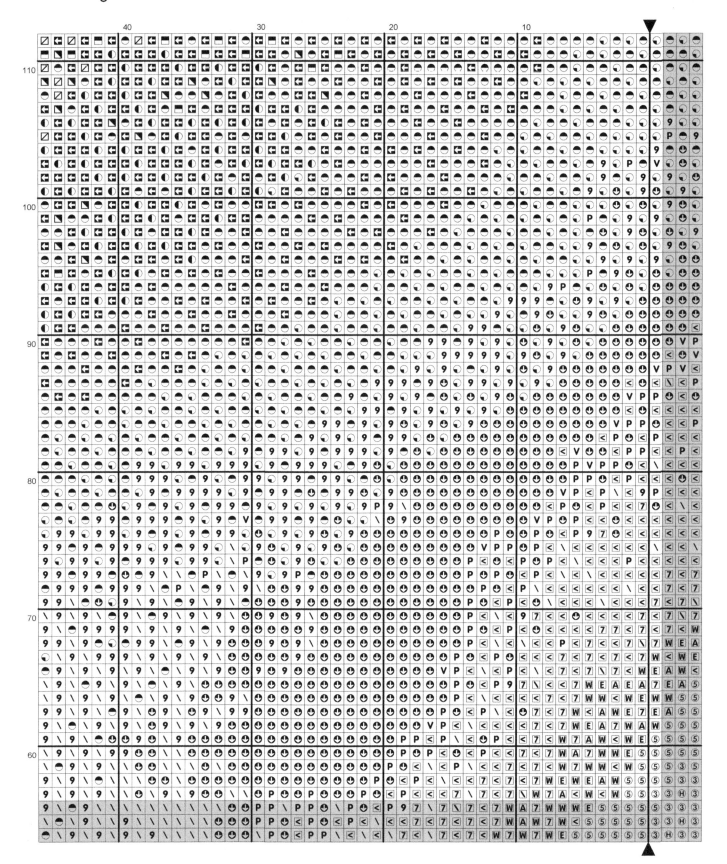

Chart Page Number 4 Nature's Finest No. 044

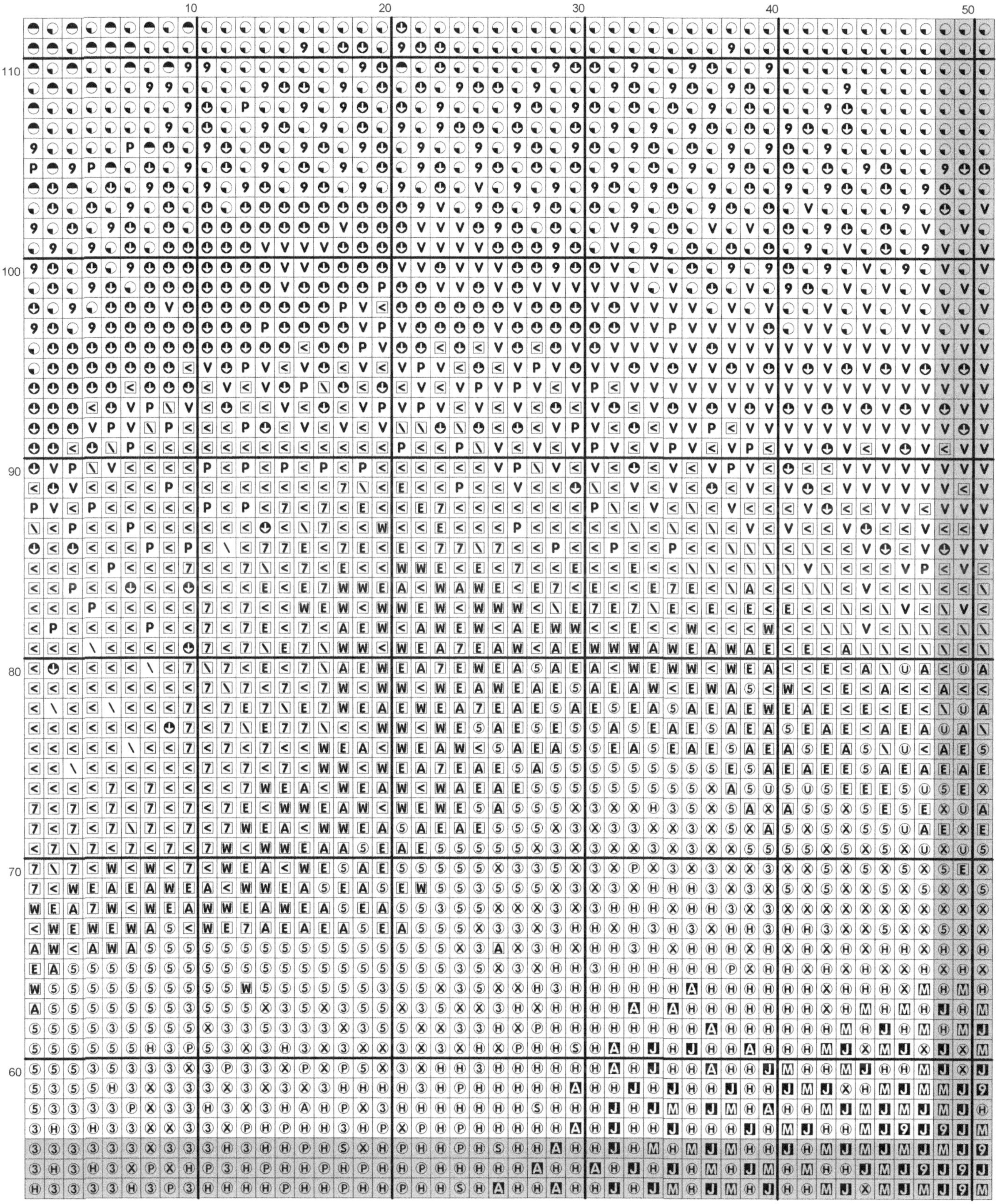

Chart Page Number 5 — Nature's Finest No. 044

Chart Page Number 6 Nature's Finest No. 044

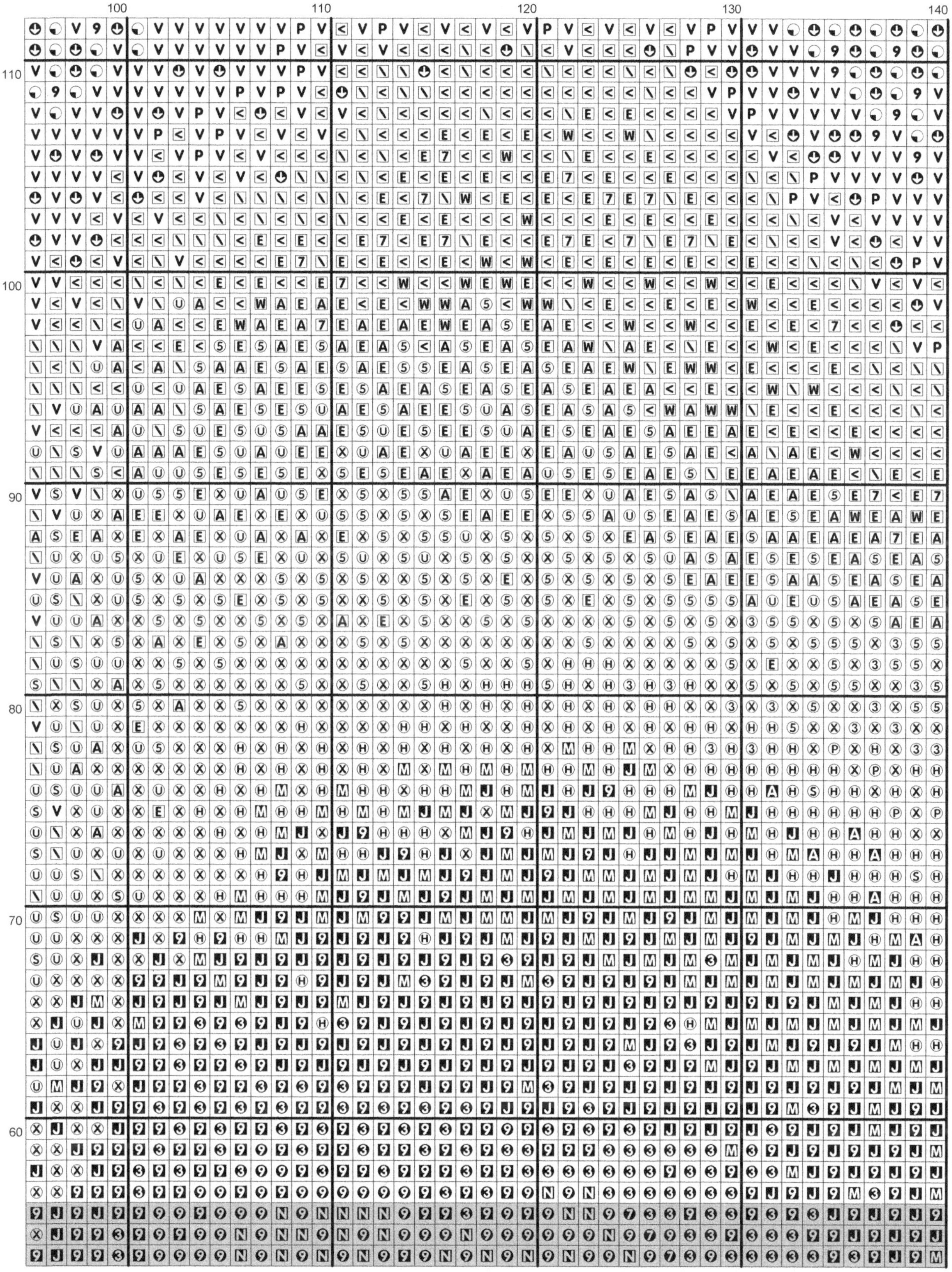

Chart Page Number 7   Nature's Finest No. 044

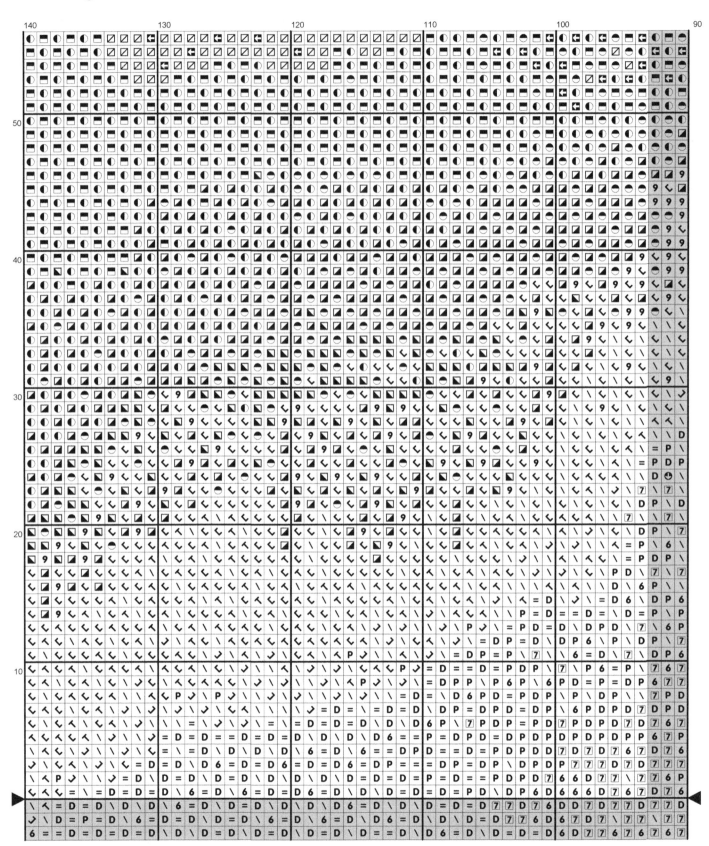

Chart Page Number 8

Nature's Finest No. 044

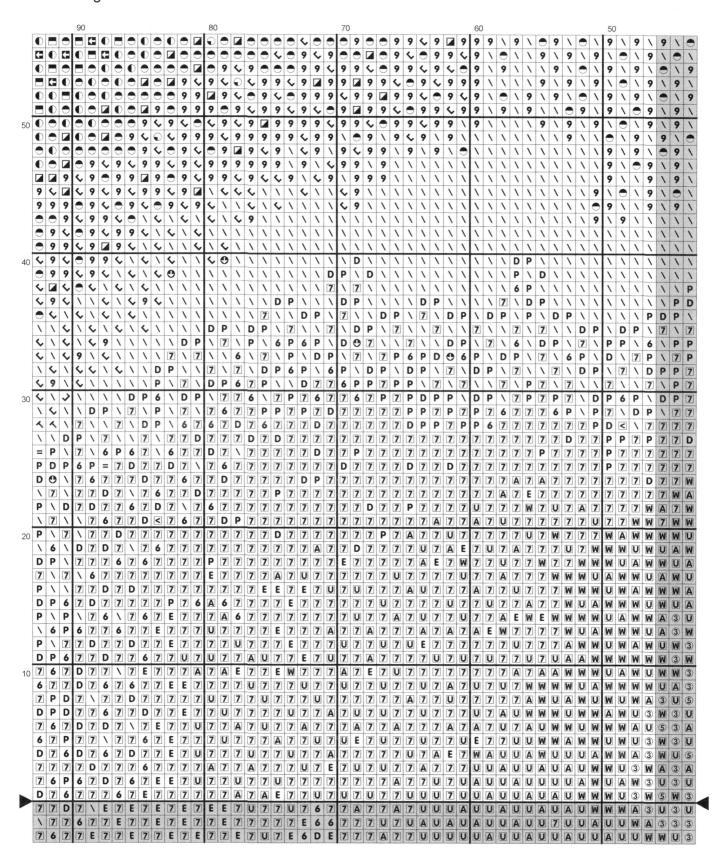

Chart Page Number 9 — Nature's Finest No. 044

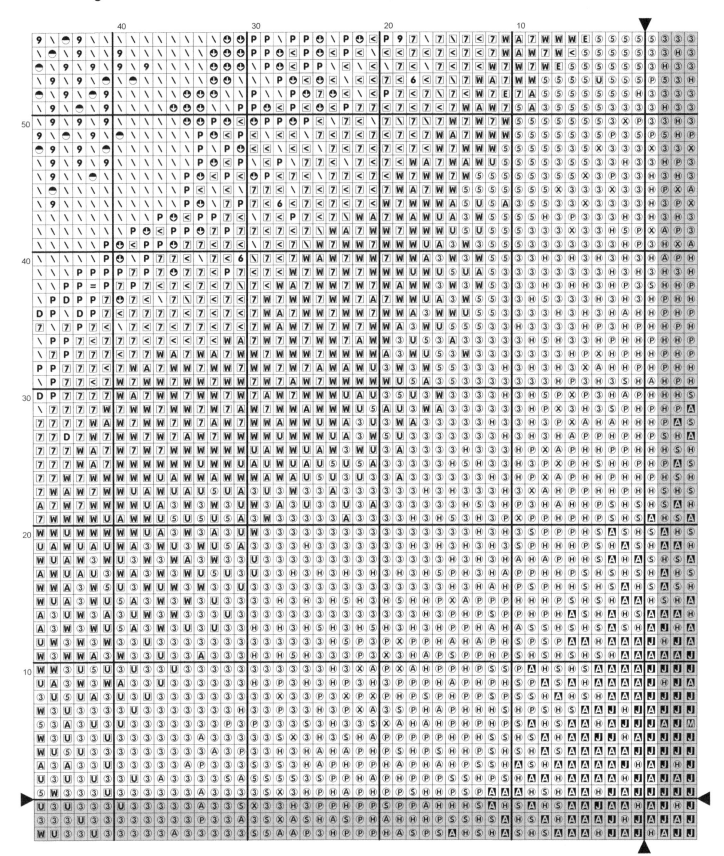

Chart Page Number 10 — Nature's Finest No. 044

Chart Page Number 11 Nature's Finest No. 044

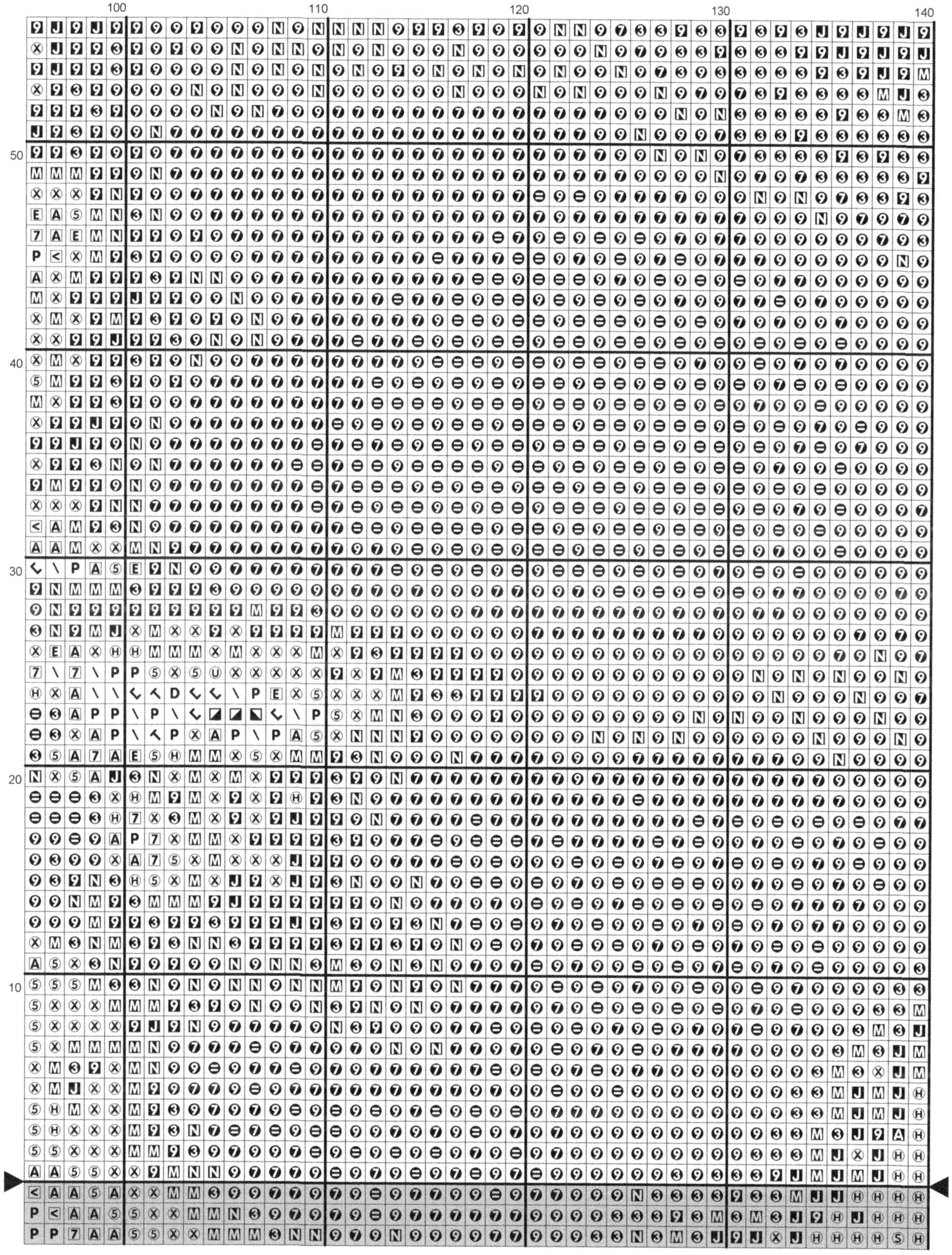
100
110
120
130
140
50
40
30
20
10

Nature's Finest No. 044

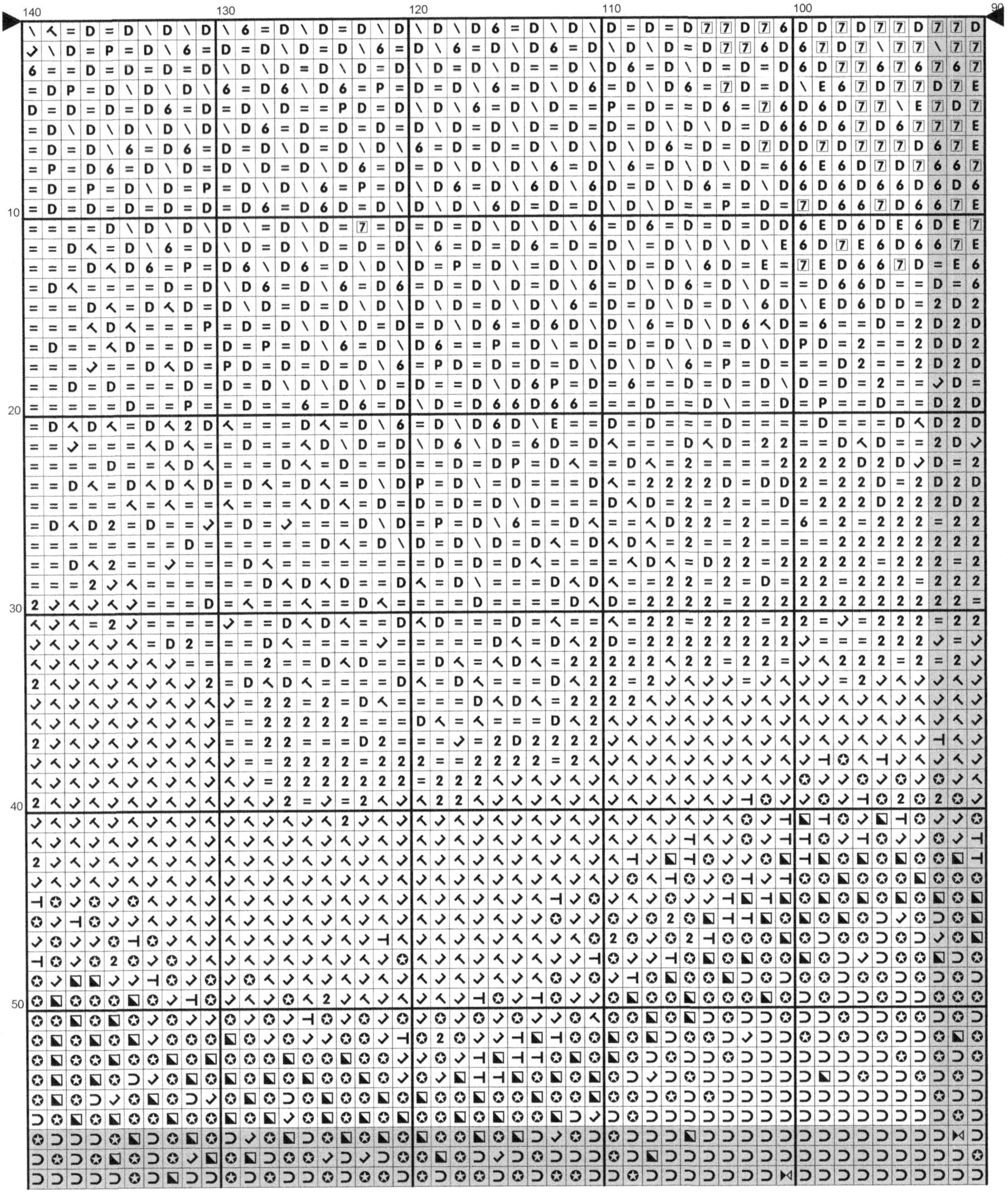

Chart Page Number 14 Nature's Finest No. 044

Chart Page Number 15 Nature's Finest No. 044

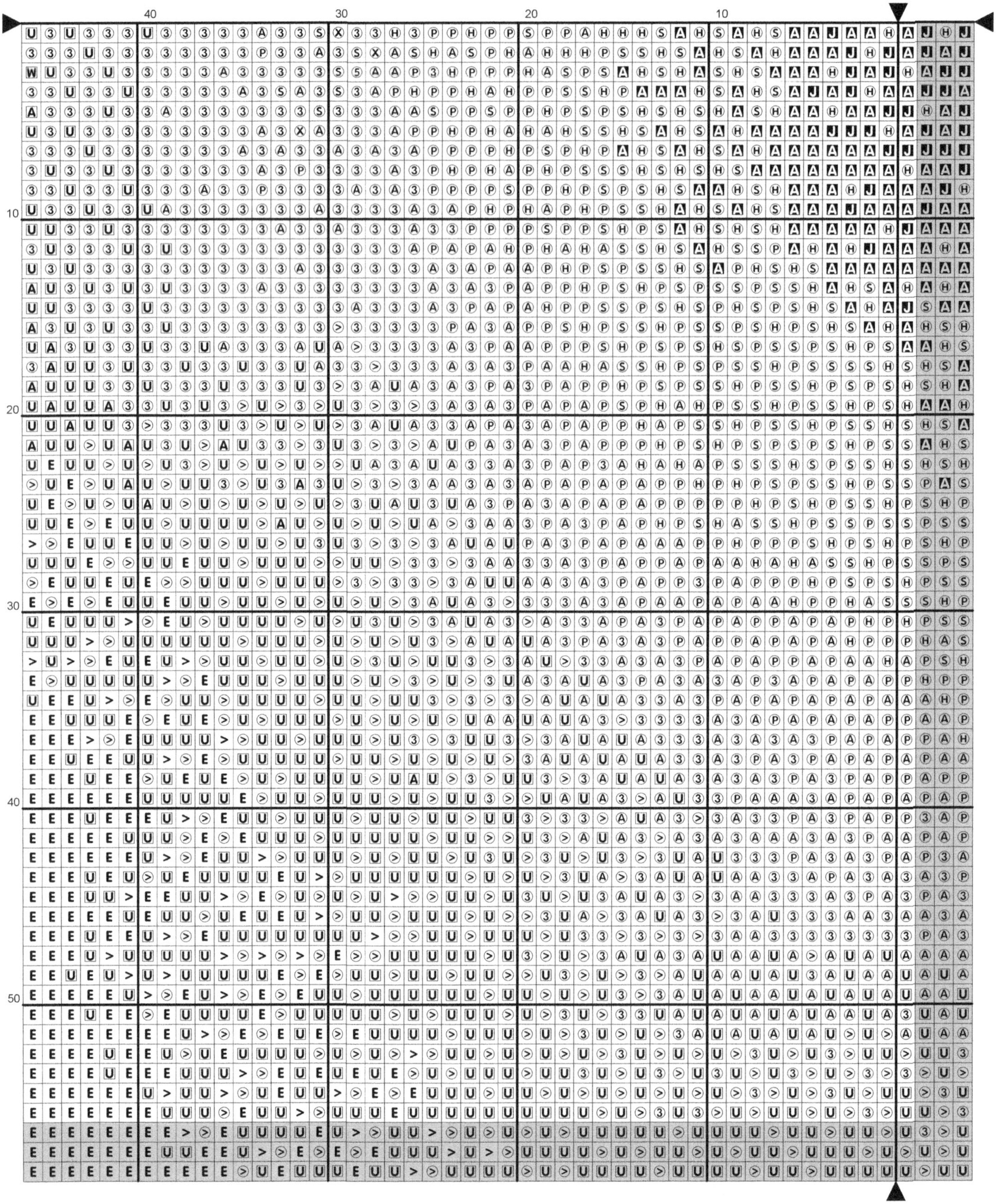

Chart Page Number 16 Nature's Finest No. 044

Chart Page Number 17   Nature's Finest No. 044

Chart Page Number 18   Nature's Finest No. 044

Chart Page Number 19   Nature's Finest No. 044

Chart Page Number 20 Nature's Finest No. 044

Chart Page Number 21   Nature's Finest No. 044

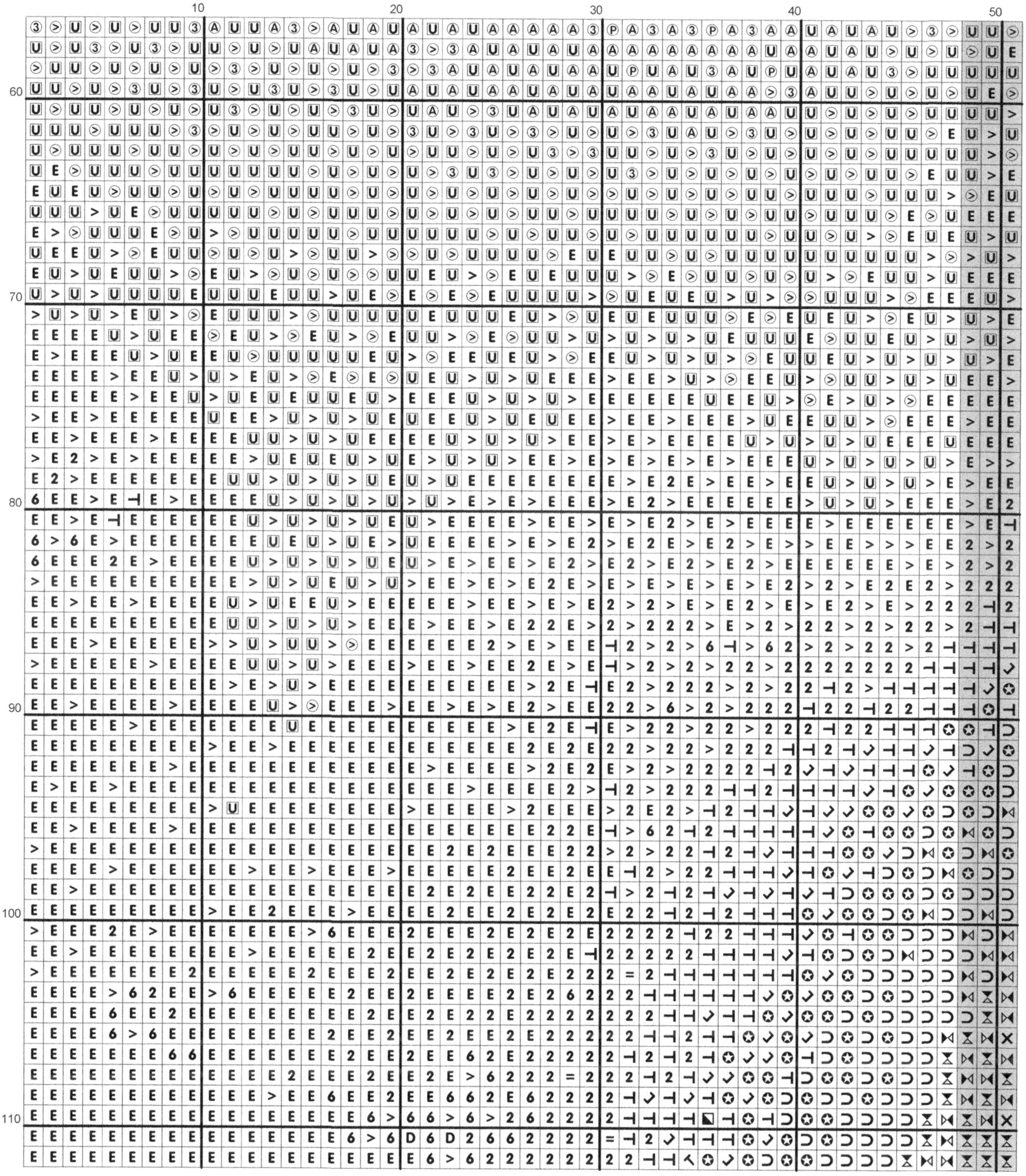
10
20
30
40
50
60
70
80
90
100
110

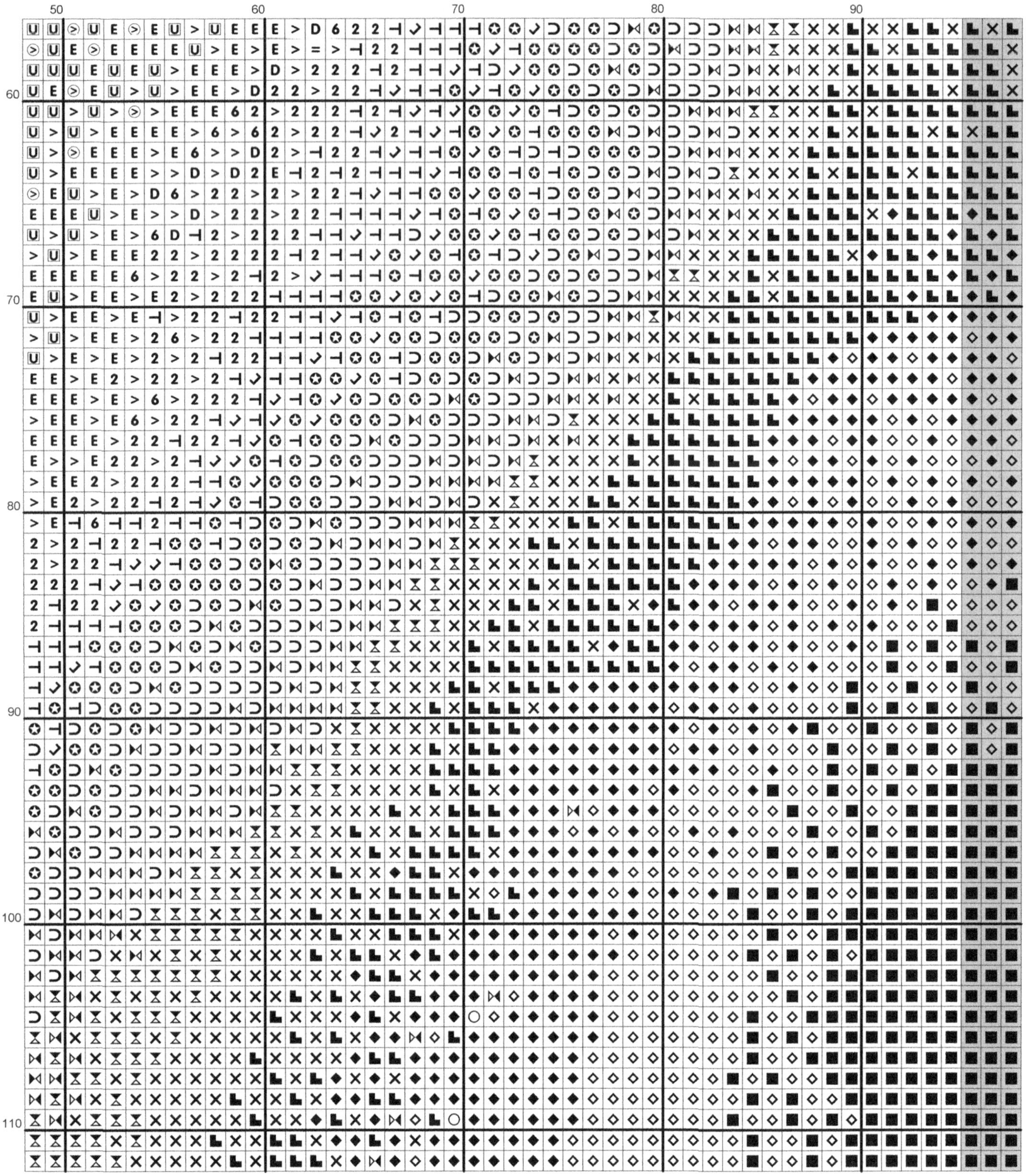
50
60
70
80
90
60
70
80
90
100
110

Chart Page Number 24   Nature's Finest No. 044

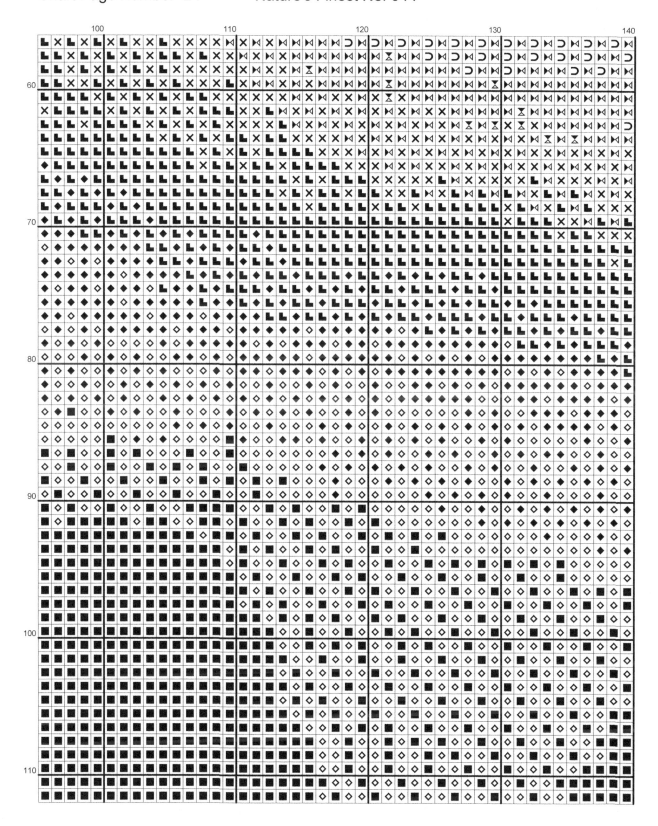

DMC FLOSS KEY

Stitch Count: 280 x 224
Size (when stitched on 14ct): 20.00 x 16.00 inches

Sym	No.	Color Name	Sym	No.	Color Name
■	310	Black	◣	370	Medium mustard
⌃	371	Green plains	P	372	Light mustard
✪	420	Hazelnut	7	422	Light oak
6	436	Teddy brown	W	437	Camel
○	501	Pond green	⇐	502	Blue green
\	612	String brown	<	613	Rope brown
◐	640	Green grey	9	642	Earth grey
Ⓤ	644	Light green grey	⬚	645	Dark steel grey
◔	647	Rock grey	③	676	Savannah gold
Ⓗ	677	Sand gold	2	680	Dark old gold
❼	712	Cream	E	729	Honey gold
⋈	732	Bronze green	⑤	738	Sahara cream
M	739	Dune cream	Ⓢ	744	Grapefruit yellow
A	745	Banana yellow	ꙮ	746	Vanillla
9	822	Cotton cream	X	829	Dark green bronze
✕	830	Green oak brown	⊃	831	Green bronze
✓	832	Light green bronze	D	833	Brass
E	842	Beige rope	⋈	869	Coffee brown
L	898	Teak brown	◆	938	Espresso brown
◪	3012	Marsh green	◐	3022	Elephant grey
V	3023	Light platinum grey	⊖	3032	Dark antique silver
⌃	3045	Coffee cream	A	3046	Rye beige
⊗	3047	Silver birch beige	Ŋ	3078	Pale yellow
▬	3363	Herb green	◇	3371	Ebony
◣	3768	Storm grey	N	3782	Gingerbread brown
⊛	3821	Straw yellow	A	3822	Light straw yellow
❸	3823	Ivory	U	3827	Beech brown
=	3828	Oaktree brown	⊣	3829	Ochre brown
>	3852	Mustard yellow	Ⓟ	3855	Autumn gold
⊖	3865	Winter white	N	ECRU	ECRU

Shopping List

DMC	Color	Qty	DMC	Color	Qty	DMC Color	Qty
310	Black	1	830	Green oak brown	1		
370	Medium mustard	1	831	Green bronze	2		
371	Green plains	1	832	Light green bronze	1		
372	Light mustard	1	833	Brass	1		
420	Hazelnut	1	842	Beige rope	1		
422	Light oak	1	869	Coffee brown	1		
436	Teddy brown	1	898	Teak brown	1		
437	Camel	1	938	Espresso brown	1		
501	Pond green	1	3012	Marsh green	1		
502	Blue green	1	3022	Elephant grey	1		
612	String brown	1	3023	Light platinum grey	1		
613	Rope brown	1	3032	Dark antique silver	1		
640	Green grey	1	3045	Coffee cream	1		
642	Earth grey	1	3046	Rye beige	1		
644	Light green grey	1	3047	Silver birch beige	1		
645	Dark steel grey	1	3078	Pale yellow	2		
647	Rock grey	1	3363	Herb green	1		
676	Savannah gold	2	3371	Ebony	1		
677	Sand gold	2	3768	Storm grey	1		
680	Dark old gold	2	3782	Gingerbread brown	1		
712	Cream	1	3821	Straw yellow	1		
729	Honey gold	2	3822	Light straw yellow	1		
732	Bronze green	1	3823	Ivory	1		
738	Sahara cream	1	3827	Beech brown	2		
739	Dune cream	1	3828	Oaktree brown	1		
744	Grapefruit yellow	1	3829	Ochre brown	1		
745	Banana yellow	1	3852	Mustard yellow	1		
746	Vanilla	1	3855	Autumn gold	1		
822	Cotton cream	1	3865	Winter white	1		
829	Dark green bronze	1	ECRU	ECRU	1		

www.stitchx.com

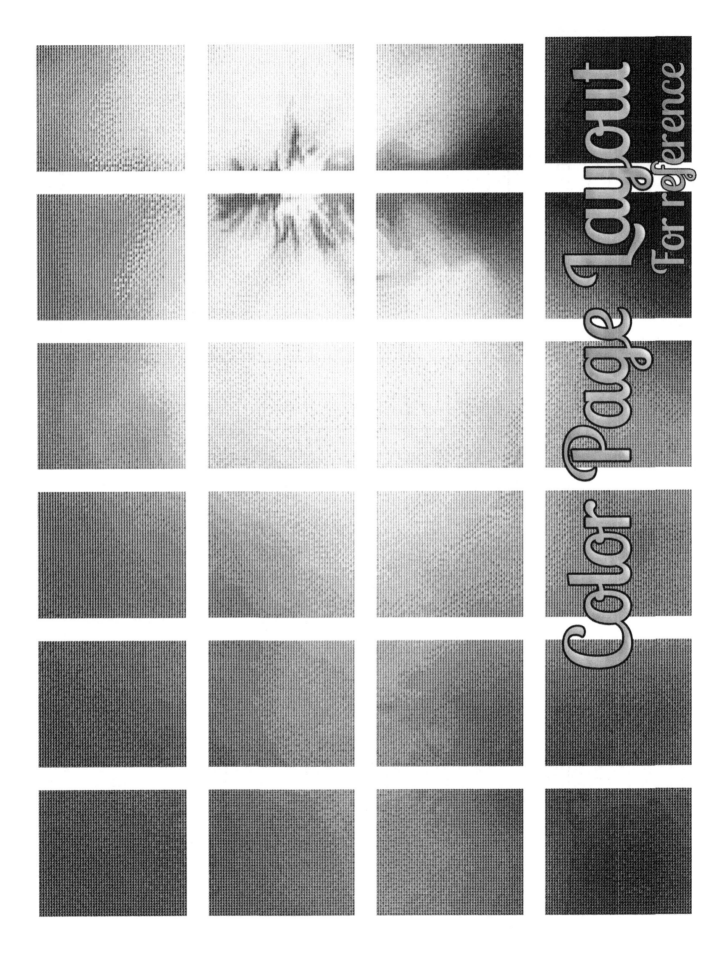

Nature's Finest Cross Stitch Pattern

Stitch Count: 280 x 224

Finished Size on 14ct Aida: 20" x 16"

www.stitchx.com

Chart Page Number 1

Nature's Finest No. 045

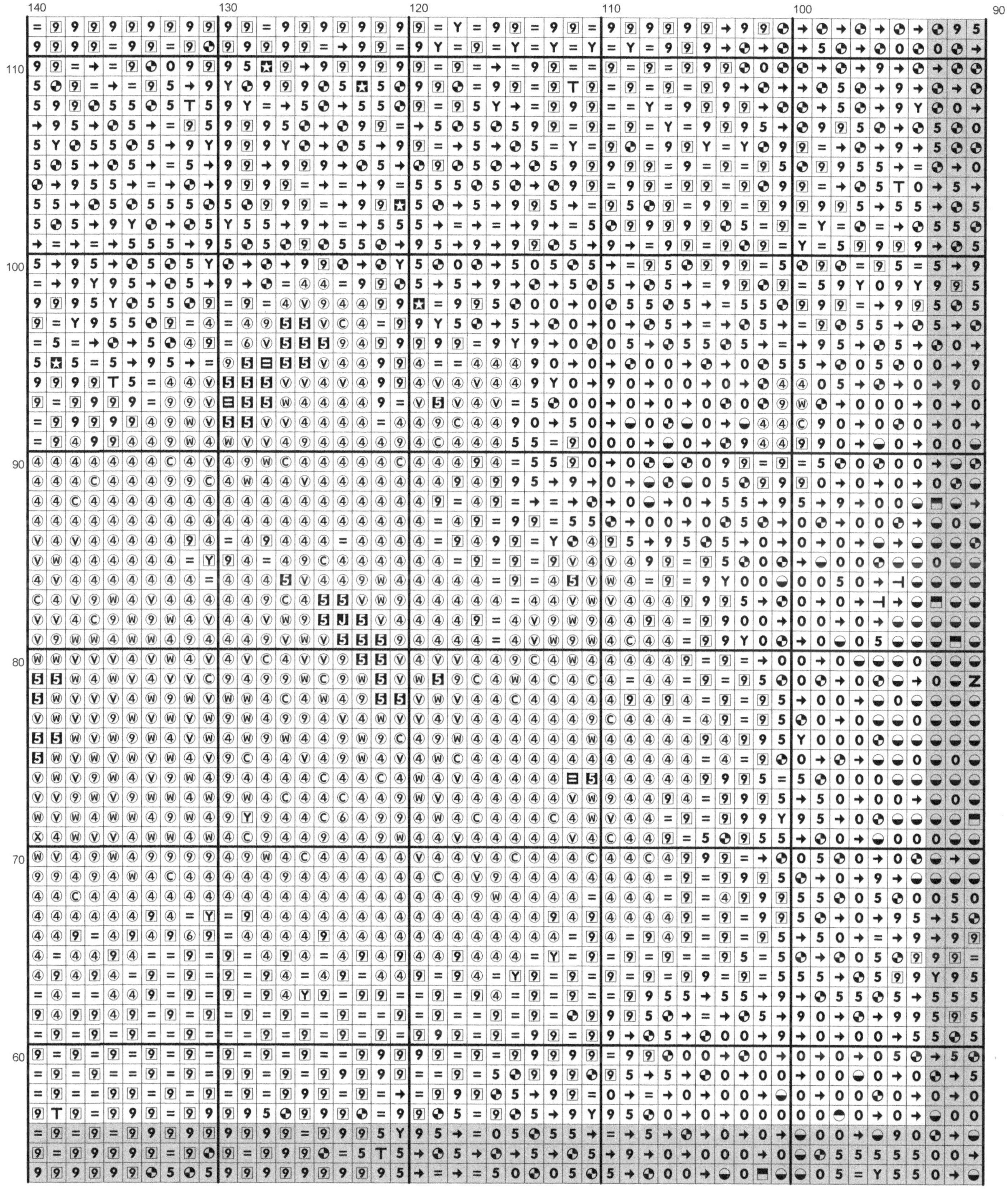

Chart Page Number 2 Nature's Finest No. 045

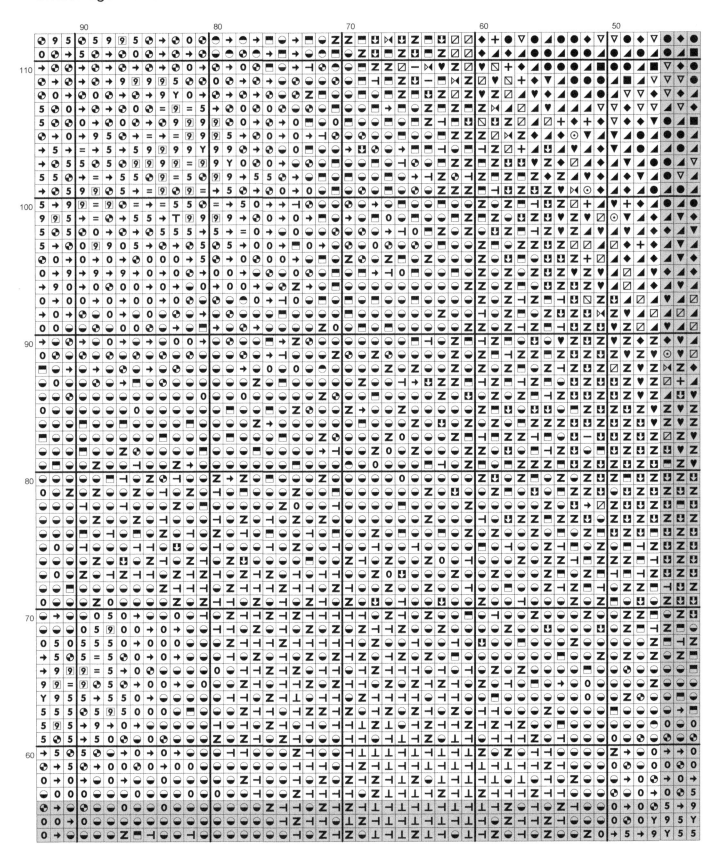

Chart Page Number 3 Nature's Finest No. 045

Chart Page Number 4　　Nature's Finest No. 045

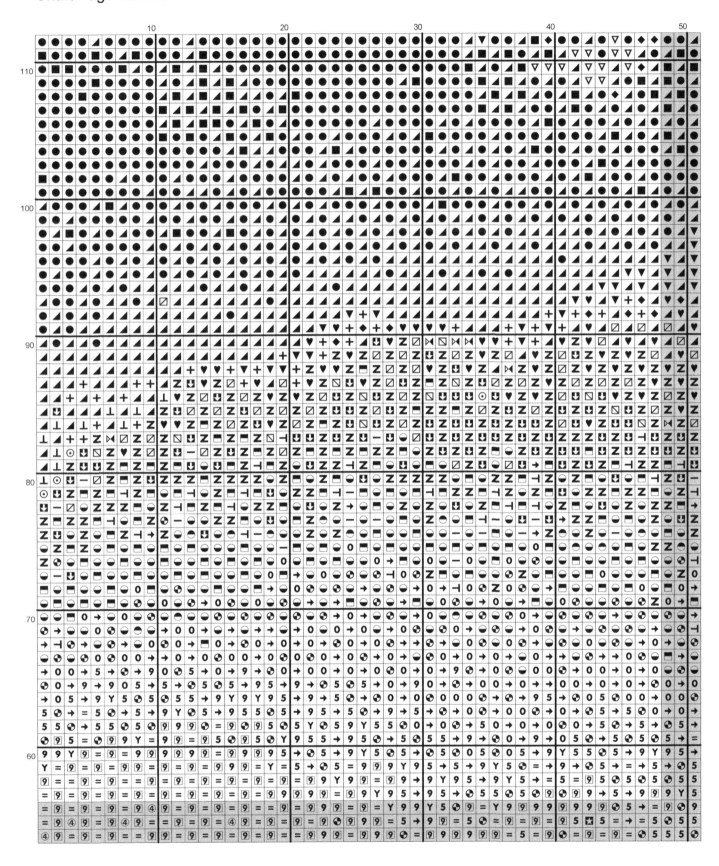

Chart Page Number 5 Nature's Finest No. 045

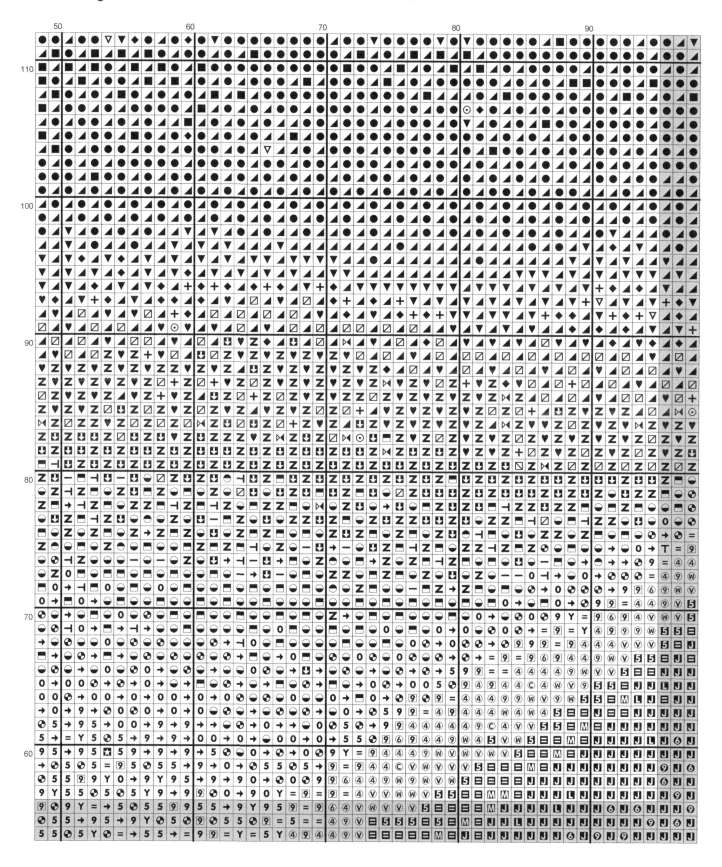

Chart Page Number 6 — Nature's Finest No. 045

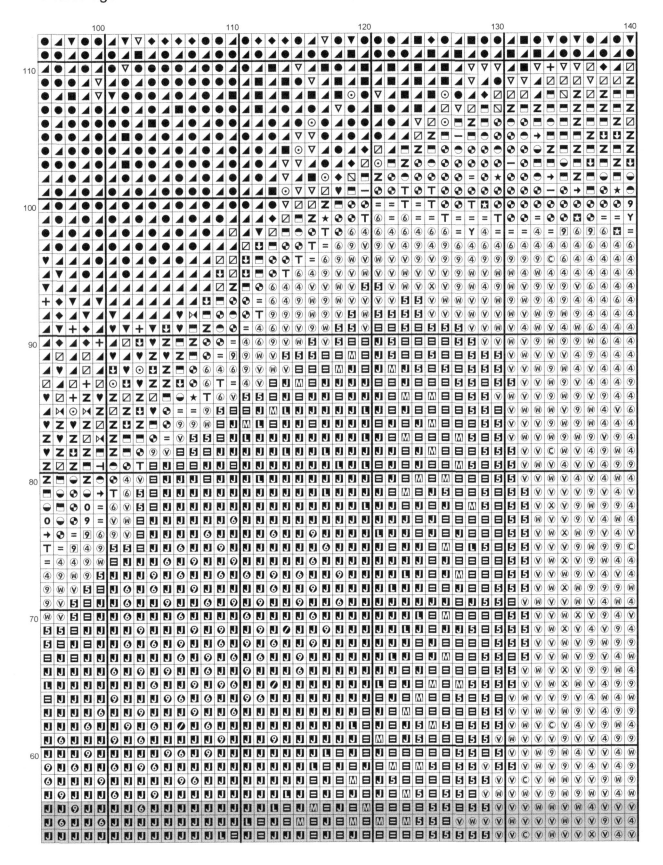

Chart Page Number 7　　Nature's Finest No. 045

Chart Page Number 8 Nature's Finest No. 045

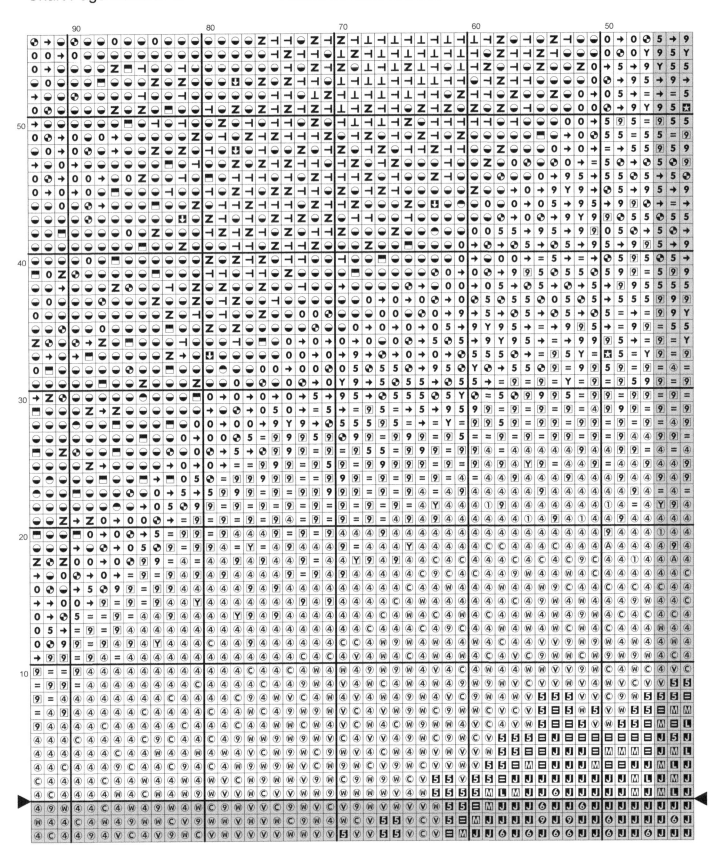

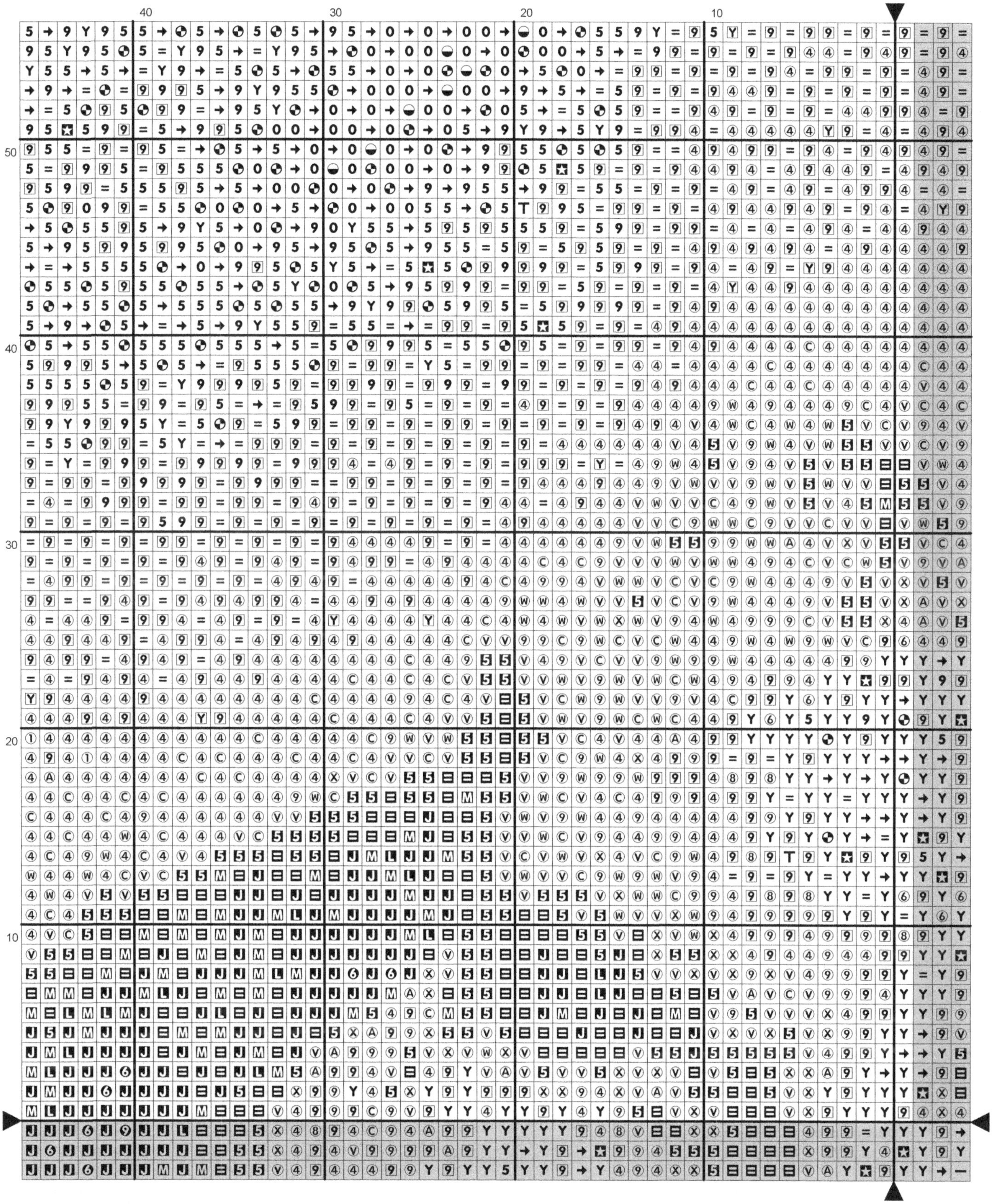

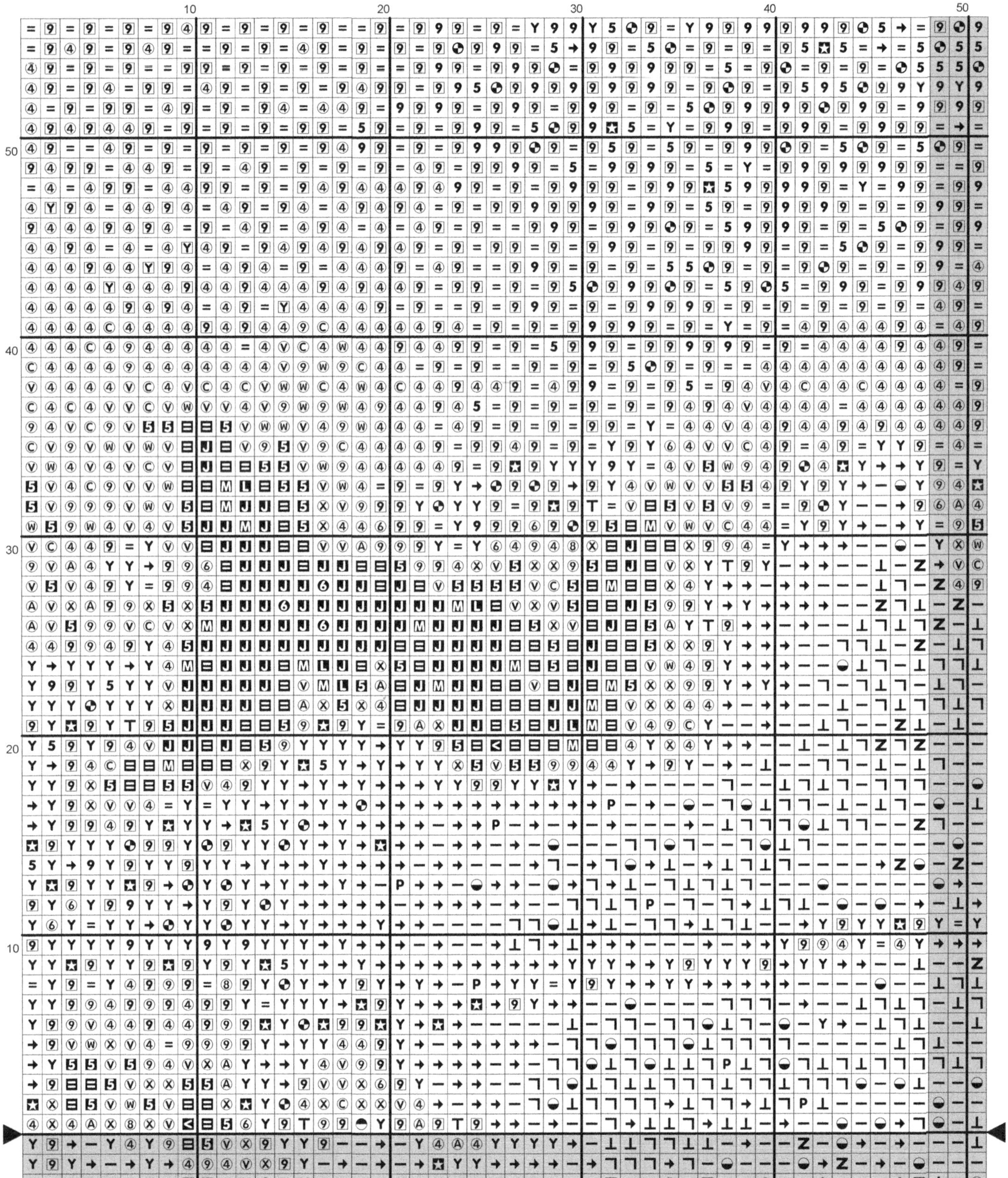
10
20
30
40
50
50
40
30
20
10

Chart Page Number 11   Nature's Finest No. 045

Chart Page Number 12   Nature's Finest No. 045

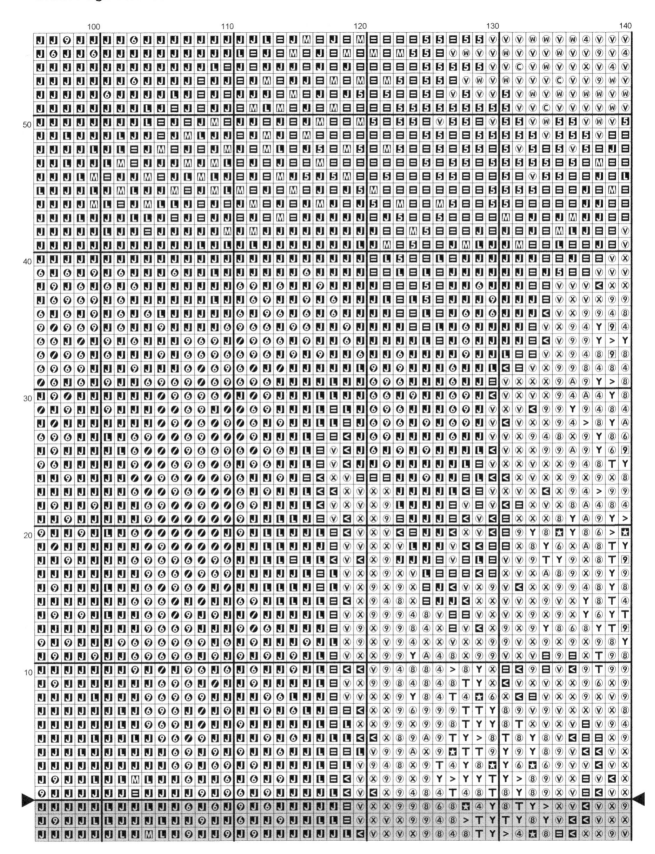

Chart Page Number 13 — Nature's Finest No. 045

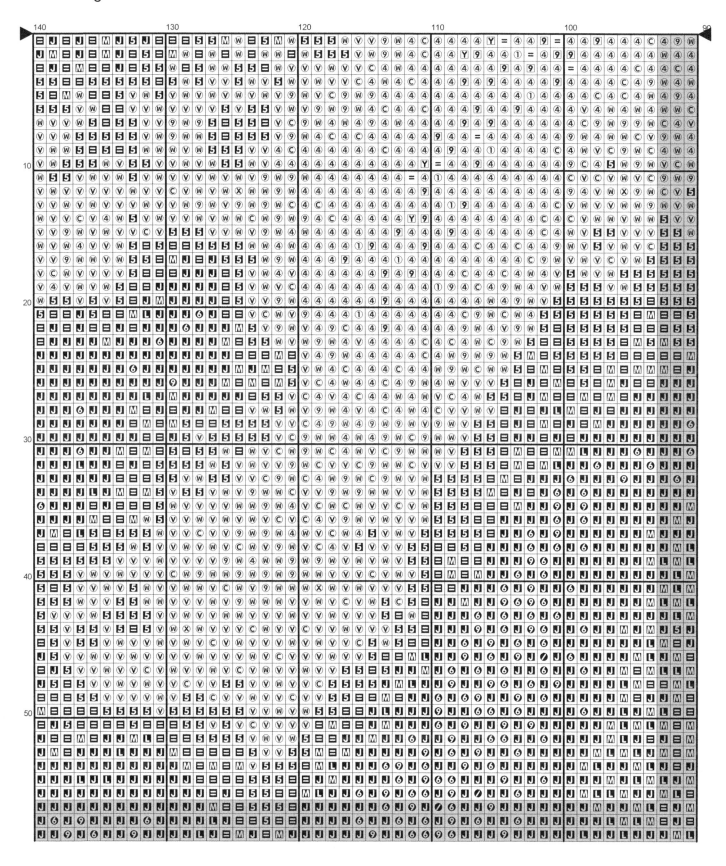

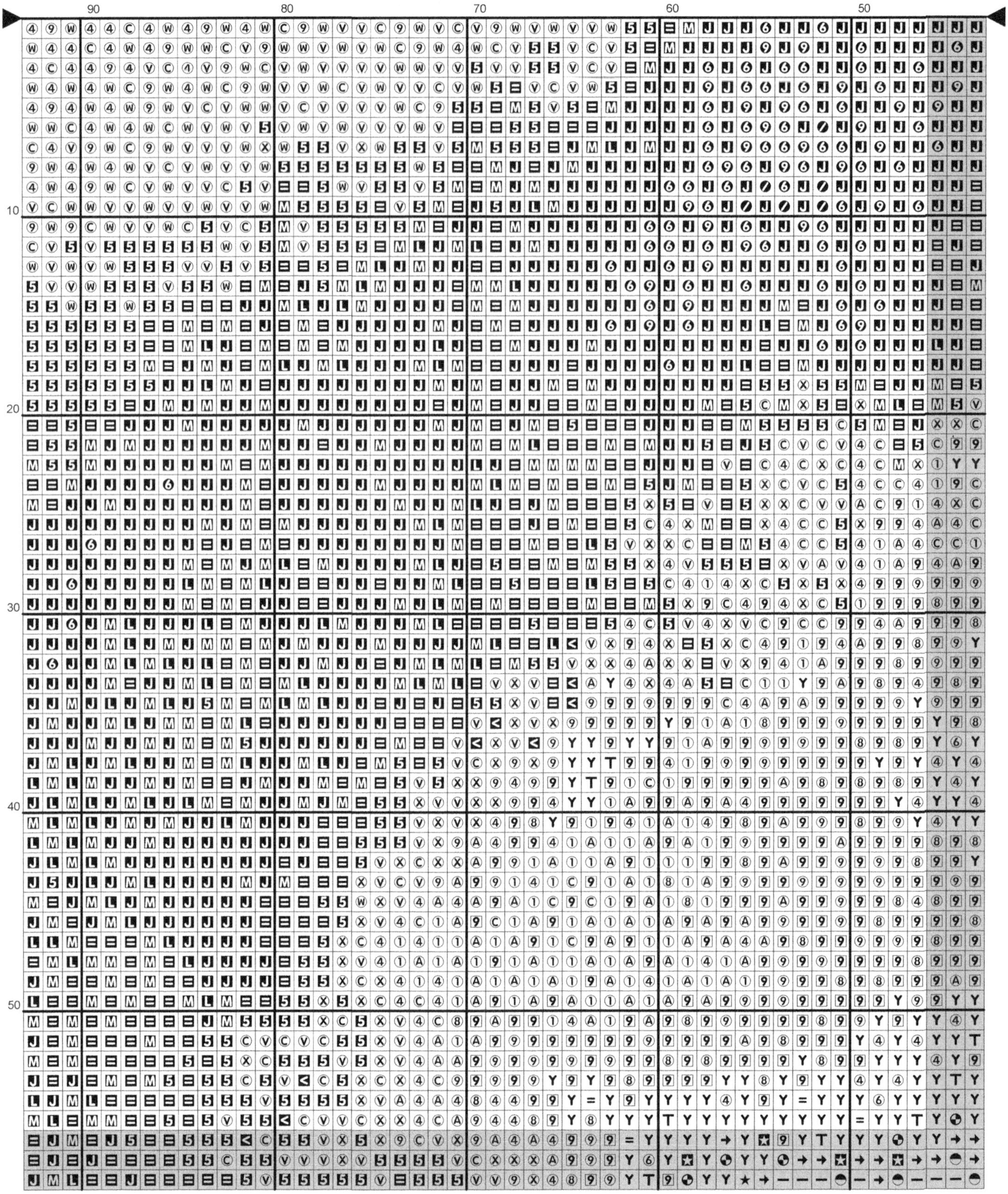
90
80
70
60
50
10
20
30
40
50

Chart Page Number 15   Nature's Finest No. 045

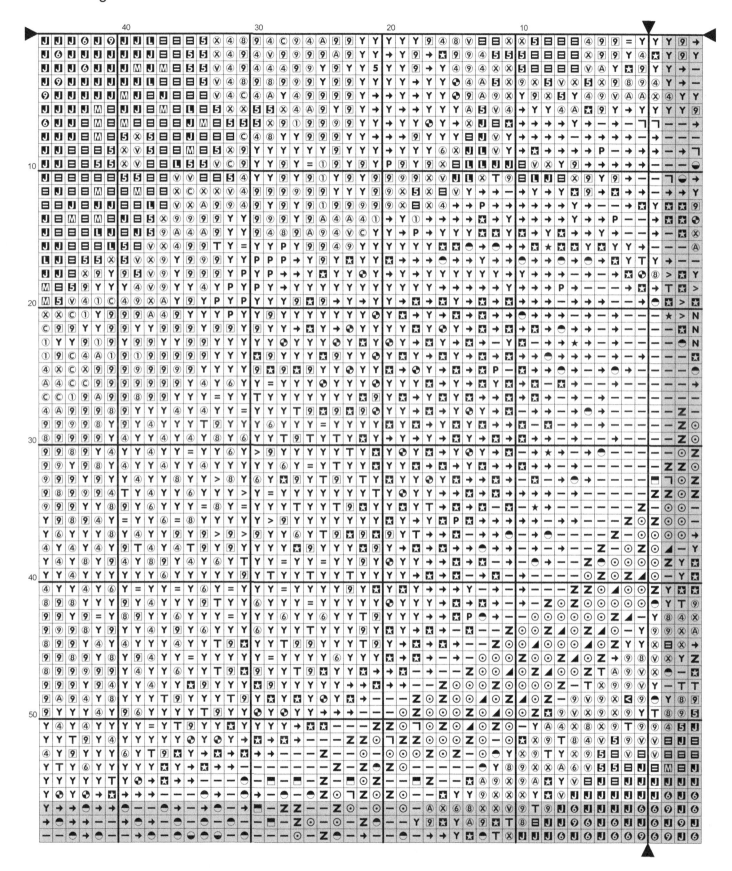

Chart Page Number 16   Nature's Finest No. 045

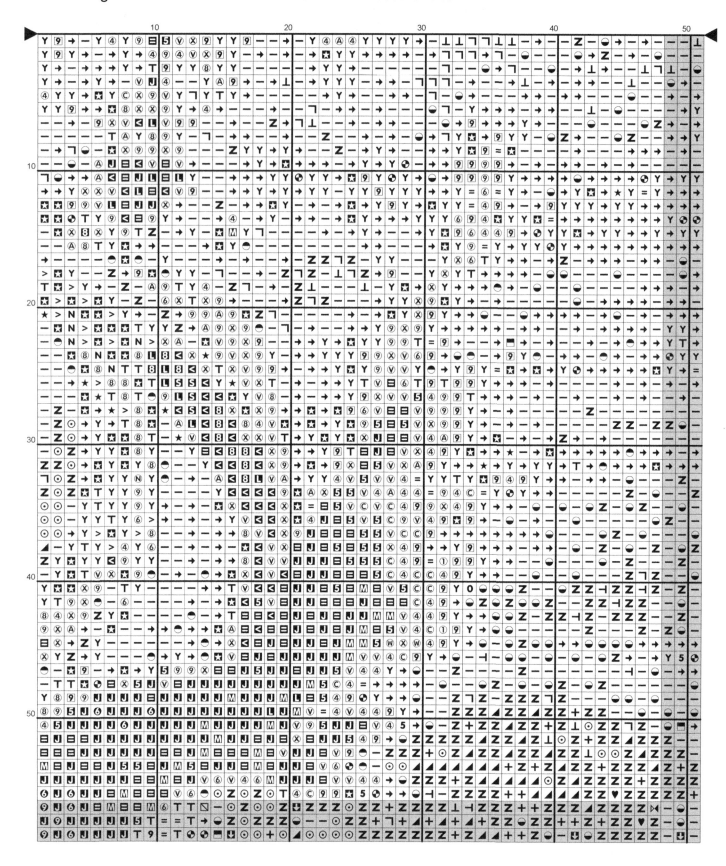

Chart Page Number 17   Nature's Finest No. 045

Chart Page Number 18   Nature's Finest No. 045

Chart Page Number 19 Nature's Finest No. 045

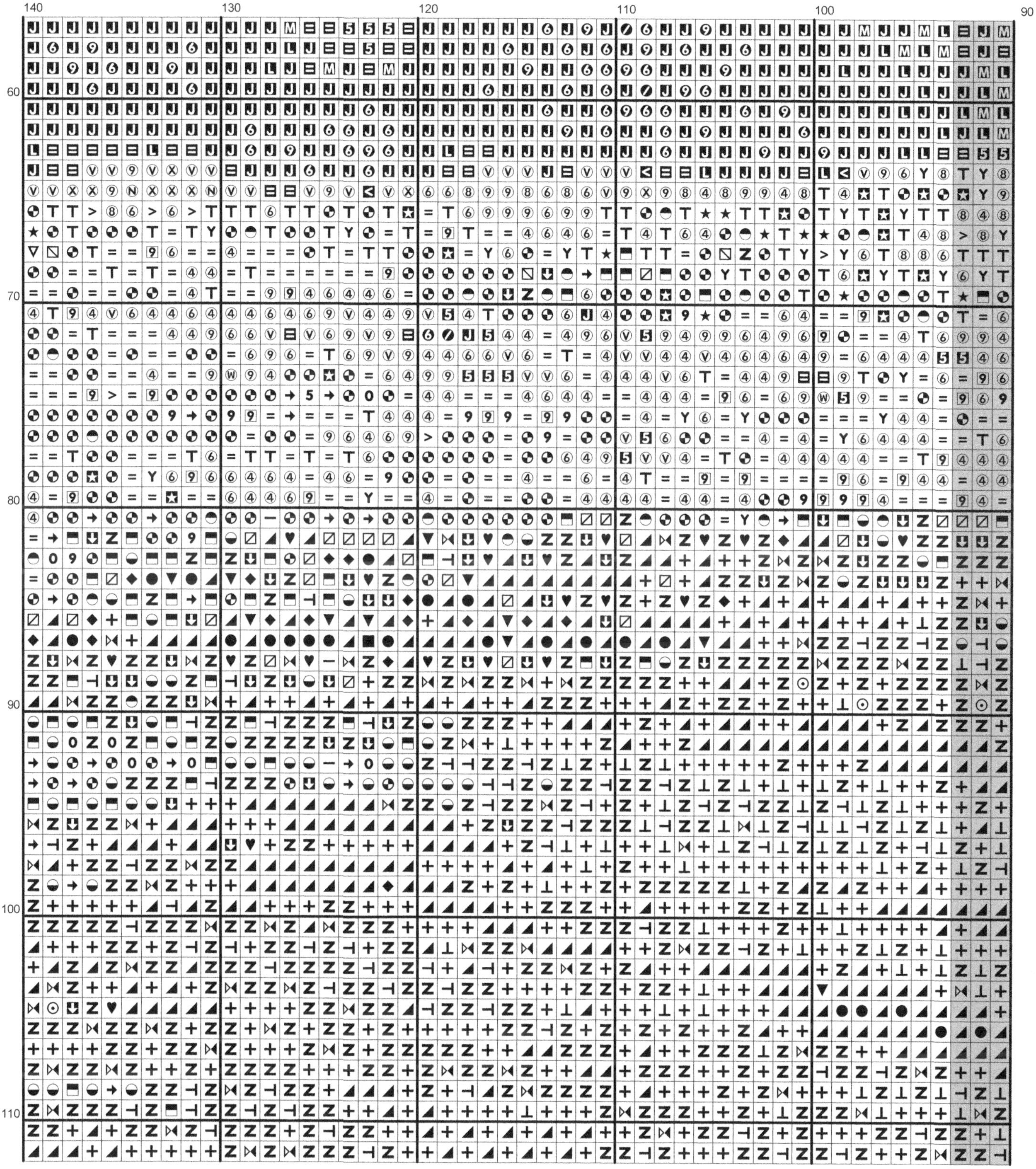

Chart Page Number 20 Nature's Finest No. 045

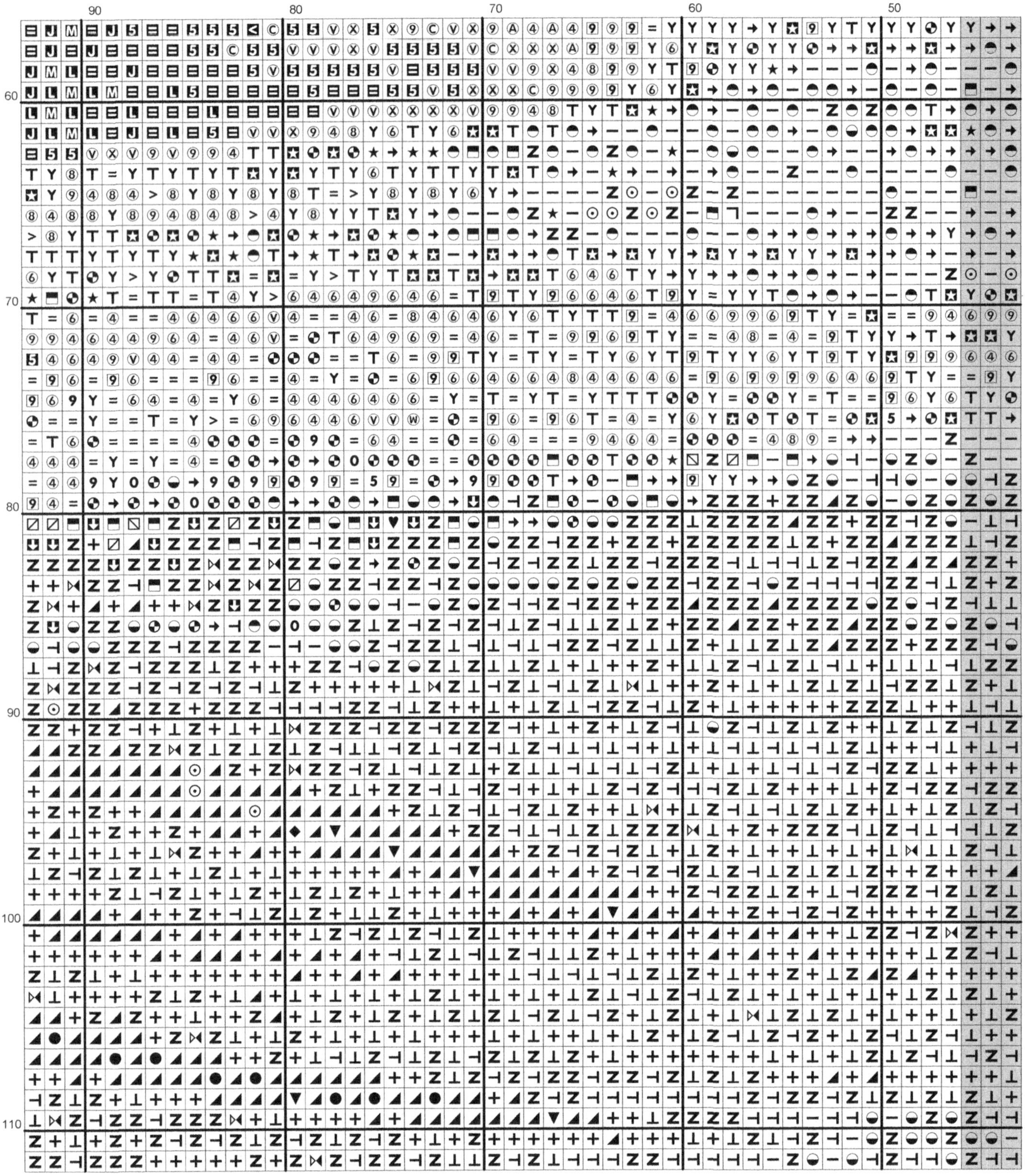

Chart Page Number 21 Nature's Finest No. 045

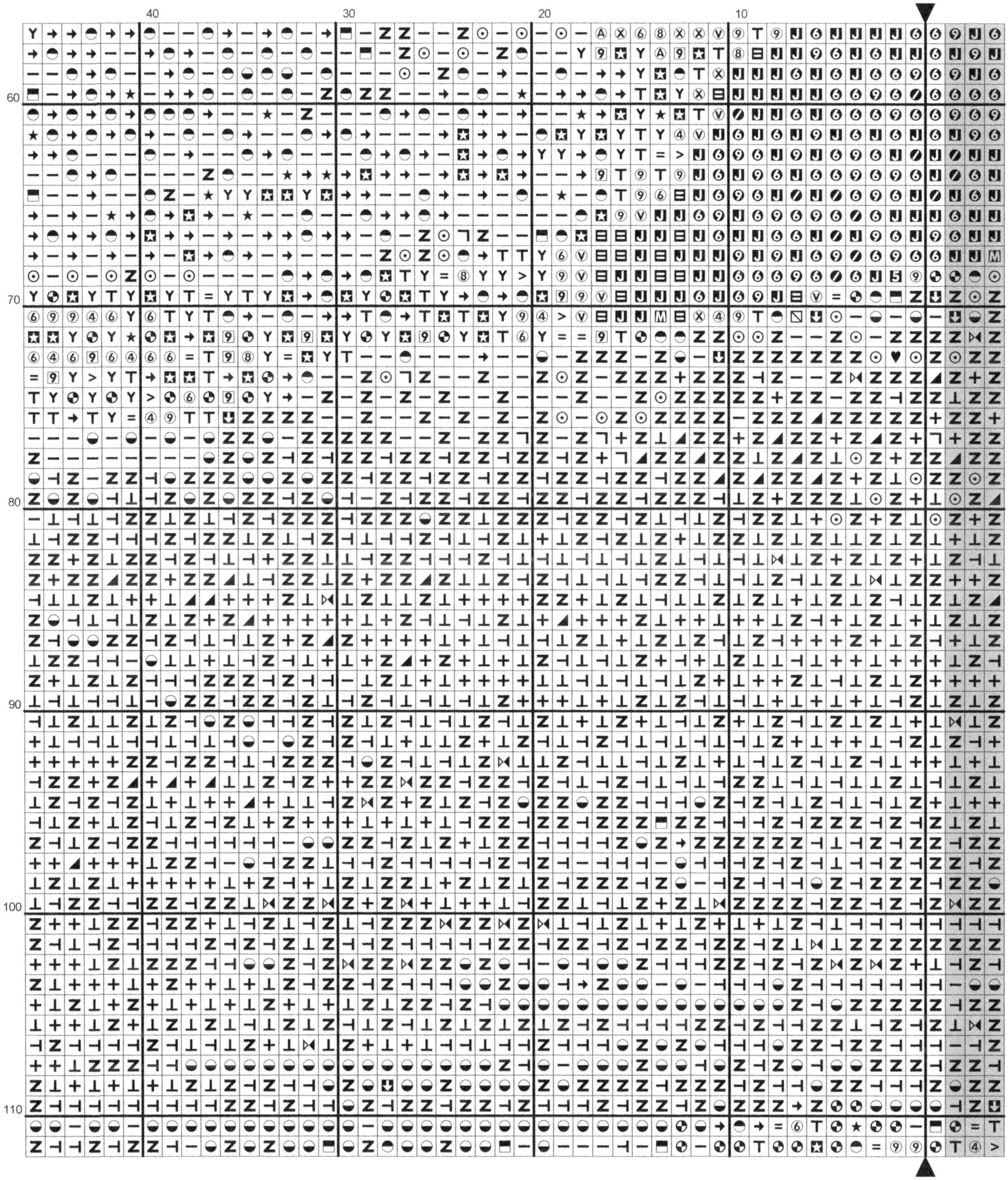

Chart Page Number 22 Nature's Finest No. 045

Chart Page Number 23   Nature's Finest No. 045

Chart Page Number 24 Nature's Finest No. 045

DMC FLOSS KEY

Stitch Count: 280 x 224
Size (when stitched on 14ct): 20.00 x 16.00 inches

Sym	No.	Color Name	Sym	No.	Color Name
ⓦ	159	Light blue grey	=	160	Storm blue
★	163	Eucalyptus green	⊟	168	Mouse grey
>	169	Pewter grey	▼	311	Dark polar blue
↧	312	Night blue	⑥	318	Granite grey
o	322	Delft blue	5	334	Pale indigo blue
N	368	Nile green	ⓥ	415	Chrome grey
⑧	503	Thyme green	◡	517	Dark wedgewood blue
⊠	561	Cypress tree green	|9|	597	Iceland blue
©	598	Lagoon turquoise	Ⓝ	648	Pepper grey
◉	712	Cream	⋈	762	Pearl grey
9	793	Medium cornflower blue	♥	803	Ink blue
P	807	Pond blue	|Y|	813	Light blue
●	823	Blueberry blue	⋈	824	Ocean blue
⊣	825	Sea blue	▽	924	Dark pearl green
T	926	Grey green	⑨	927	Oyster grey
◂	928	Light pearl grey	⊠	930	Slate grey
◕	931	Blue grey	④	932	Seagull blue
■	939	Dark navy blue	⊙	991	Dark aquamarine green
8	3024	Pale steel grey	S	3033	Antique silver
L	3072	Pale pearl grey	◆	3750	Deep petrol blue
5	3752	Light porcelain blue	M	3753	Moonlight blue
6	3756	Cloud blue	⊥	3765	Dark medium blue
①	3766	Light medium blue	▬	3768	Storm grey
◢	3808	Petrol blue	Z	3809	Deep turquoise
→	3810	Dark turquoise	ⓧ	3813	Light green
⌐	3814	Spruce green	◔	3815	Eucalyptus Green
✪	3816	Snake green	Ⓐ	3817	Polar tree green
+	3842	Deep Wedgewood blue	—	3848	Medium teal green
Y	3849	Green turquoise	∅	3865	Winter white

Shopping List

DMC Color		Qty	DMC Color		Qty	DMC Color		Qty
159	Light blue grey	1	928	Light pearl grey	1			
160	Storm blue	1	930	Slate grey	1			
163	Eucalyptus green	1	931	Blue grey	2			
168	Mouse grey	2	932	Seagull blue	2			
169	Pewter grey	1	939	Dark navy blue	1			
311	Dark polar blue	1	991	Dark aquamarine green	1			
312	Night blue	1	3024	Pale steel grey	1			
318	Granite grey	1	3033	Antique silver	1			
322	Delft blue	1	3072	Pale pearl grey	1			
334	Pale indigo blue	1	3750	Deep petrol blue	1			
368	Nile green	1	3752	Light porcelain blue	1			
415	Chrome grey	2	3753	Moonlight blue	1			
503	Thyme green	1	3756	Cloud blue	1			
517	Dark wedgewood blue	2	3765	Dark medium blue	1			
561	Cypress tree green	1	3766	Light medium blue	1			
597	Iceland blue	2	3768	Storm grey	1			
598	Lagoon turquoise	1	3808	Petrol blue	3			
648	Pepper grey	1	3809	Deep turquoise	3			
712	Cream	1	3810	Dark turquoise	2			
762	Pearl grey	4	3813	Light green	1			
793	Medium cornflower b	1	3814	Spruce green	1			
803	Ink blue	1	3815	Eucalyptus Green	1			
807	Pond blue	1	3816	Snake green	1			
813	Light blue	1	3817	Polar tree green	1			
823	Blueberry blue	2	3842	Deep Wedgewood blue	1			
824	Ocean blue	1	3848	Medium teal green	2			
825	Sea blue	1	3849	Green turquoise	2			
924	Dark pearl green	1	3865	Winter white	1			
926	Grey green	1						
927	Oyster grey	1						

www.stitchx.com

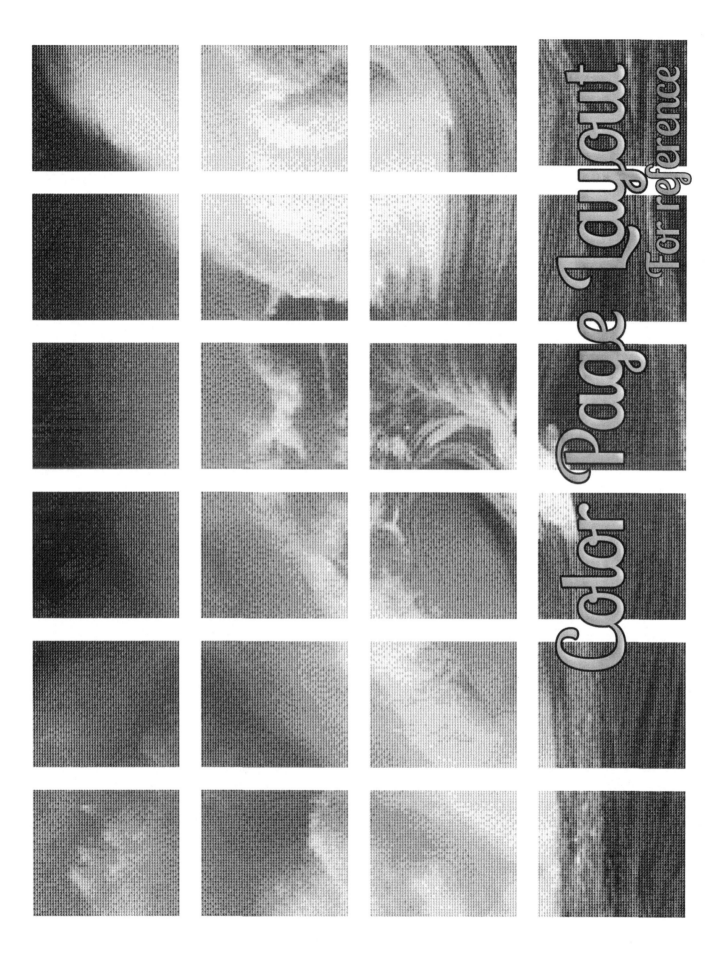

Cross Stitch Project Planner

Pattern Name:_____

Designer:_____

Fabric color I plan to use:_____

Count of fabric I plan to use: _____

Fabric size calculations:

What is the stitch count of my pattern:

*A*_____ x *B*_____

What count is my fabric? If using aida cloth, or stitching "over one", enter the amount in blank *C*. If using linen or evenweave and stitching "over two", divide that number by 2. (Example: For 28 count fabric, divide by 2, and enter '14' in blank *C*)

*C*_____

To figure the finished design size, divide the stitch count by your fabric count. Find the values from the blanks above and do the calculations here:

A _____ divided by *C* _____ = *D* _____ inches

B _____ divided by *C* _____ = *E* _____ inches

My finished **design size** will be *D* x *E*, but I will need to add extra fabric to each side to allow for framing. Most framers like to have an extra 3-4 inches on each side. (This also helps if I accidentally stitch my design off center a bit.)

How much fabric do I want to add to each side? *F* _____ inches

Now, multiply this by two. *F* _____ x 2 = *G* _____ inches

Add this to my finished design size that I figured earlier (*D* x *E*).

D _____ inches + *G* _____ inches = *H* _____ inches length

E _____ inches + *G* _____ inches = *I* _____ inches width

The fabric size that I need for my project is:

_____ x _____ **inches**

Made in the USA
Middletown, DE
04 March 2022